China: An A–Z

by
Kai Strittmatter

Translated from the German by
Stefan Tobler

ArmchairTraveller

Copyright © 2006 Kai Strittmatter
Translation copyright © 2006 Stefan Tobler

First published in Great Britain in 2006 by Haus Publishing
Limited, 26 Cadogan Court, Draycott Avenue, London SW3 3BX

The moral rights of the author have been asserted.

A CIP catalogue record for this book is available from the
British Library

ISBN 1-904950-80-9

Typeset in Garamond 3 by MacGuru Ltd
Printed and bound by Graphicom in Vicenza, Italy
Jacket illustrations courtesy of Getty Images

始 *Shi*

The start ...

... of this book is where Chinese books traditionally end. For thousands of years the Chinese have read from right to left, in other words: from the back to the front. Which is rubbish really, because what is the back for us is the front for them. When Chinese people smile for the photographer they don't say 'cheese' in English but rather 'aubergine' in Chinese. They don't 'eat' their soup, they 'drink' it, and not before, but after the meal. Yet their surnames come first, not their first names first. The heart, for them, is the seat of reason, and white is the colour of mourning. They call America the 'Land of Beauty', England the 'Land of Heroes' and Germany the 'Land of Virtue'.

High time for a compass!

指南针 *Zhi nan zhen*

The Compass
Opposites meet in the end

A Chinese invention, like football, the printing press and paper (all from ancient China), as well as fruit salad with pink mayonnaise (Beijing, 21st century). Like all Chinese gadgets it has been shamelessly stolen and imitated by the West, although the West has yet to crack its clever copy protection. Actually, the West hasn't even noticed it yet. Here the secret shall be revealed. Well, actually two secrets:

1. The pink in pink mayonnaise will look even more impressive if you go for the cheap bright red Chinese ketchup from your local neighbourhood store and mix it with the mayonnaise.

2. The compass points south.

Zhi nan zhen means the 'needle that points south' and for hundreds of years the Chinese have been sniggering into their beards whenever they see a Westerner walking northwards, compass in hand. They might use the same needle, but in its interpretation the East and the West diametrically oppose each other. Something similar happens when the two engage in conversation: they use the same words, but each one's thoughts fly in opposite directions. *Communism* is one of these tricky words, sometimes *love* is too.

So will China and the West ever meet? Why not – after all, as long as the earth is round, those walking north and those walking south are bound to bump into each other.

中文 *Zhong wen*

Chinese
Foreign Characters

I once had an encounter in a train in Bavaria with a young man who collapsed drunkenly into his seat. He then proceeded to make rude remarks to the American couple across the aisle, before throwing up beside their backpack as a parting gesture.

I find it a rather unpleasant thought that by some coincidence those unfortunate Americans were actually travel writers and that in the near future a new book about Germany would appear on the shelves, featuring my drunken compatriot as an example of a typical Bavarian. On second thoughts … Anyone who has the audacity to draw sweeping conclusions from one-off experiences and encounters is treading

4

on thin ice. For that reason I'd like to start with replies to seven enduring clichés about China. Cross-cultural understanding is something wonderful, not only because it provides an opportunity to meet many good-looking foreigners bearing the enticing label 'exotic', but above all because it contributes to 'dispelling prejudices'.

I would ask you to accompany me, dear reader, in the pursuit of this worthy custom. Let us consider it a kind of preventative penance for all the sins that I will commit in the following chapters. What I now present is nothing more than a collection of fairy tales. The reader is advised to delete them from the 'I'd say off-the-top-of-my head' region of your brain:

1. *'The Chinese always eat rice.'* – The last time I went for dinner at my favourite noodle restaurant I counted well over a dozen kinds of hand-made pasta before finally giving up. It was only in medieval times that Italians smuggled noodles to Europe to make pirate copies thereof.
2. *'There are only two flavours in China: sweet and sour.'* –

On their way home the above-mentioned Italians unfortunately lost the rest of China's cuisine, which is why to this day Chinese restaurants across Europe are places of unspeakable sadness.

3. *'The Chinese are reserved, quiet, polite and modest.'* – This is a mix-up: anyone who says that is actually talking about the Japanese. If in future you run across a group of boisterous East Asians making as much racket as a county fair, you may safely assume they are Chinese.

4. *'The Chinese can't pronounce the "r" sound, and use the "l" sound instead.'* – I have met Chinese who can roll their 'r's so roundly that you dive for cover to escape the approaching thunderstorm. But it is certainly true that they do without the raw 'r' sound in their own language.

5. *'All Chinese look the same.'* – This pairs nicely with a favourite Chinese cliché about us: 'All Europeans look the same.'

6. *'China is a communist country.'* – False.

7. *'China is a capitalist country.'* – False.

So what is China then? Not so fast, I have one more prejudice to clear up: *'Chinese is a difficult language.'* That is a myth that Chinese speakers are keen to cultivate too, thus ensuring their listeners are suitably impressed. It is, of course, nonsense. There are 1.3 billion people in China of widely varying intelligence who have managed to learn Chinese, and very fluently at that. I would even propose that Chinese is one of the easiest languages on earth. I'm talking about spoken Chinese. This language manages to get by practically without any use of grammar, certainly without all those thorny conjugations and thistly declensions. It travels without any cases or those pesky tenses that plague anyone attempting cross-border flirting, cursing or haggling in Europe. Impossible? Not at all. If you want to say in Chinese that something happened yesterday, you just add the word 'yesterday' to your sentence. The poor verb can be left in peace.

Its reputation as a language that can't be learnt is partly due to one fact: Every word in the official Chinese language – which we know as Mandarin –

can be pronounced in four different tones – and each tone gives the word a completely different meaning. Tongue-twisters are often trotted out for gobsmacked novices, such as the famous '*Ma ma ma ma ma?*'. As long as you use the right tones you'll be saying 'Is the pockmarked mother nagging the nag?' Don't be put off, the tones aren't half as bad as they seem at first sight, and even horse-owners can easily avoid embarrassment, just as long as they make sure that they only entrust their horse to a mother next door who hasn't had smallpox.

It is true that among the Chinese also there is a general assumption that the mastery of their language is part of their genetic inheritance and that other people's ancestry in some way denies them the ability. Particularly in outlying regions the foreigner can easily find that when asking for directions in Chinese, he or she will be met with a blank stare. Why? Because what tripped off the foreigner's tongue obviously could not have been Chinese. I have often had my repeated questions answered with a laconic 'I'm sorry, we don't speak English.' Of course that might also have been a polite comment on the fluency of my Mandarin.

This is an interesting psychological reaction, which works just as well the other way round. In *East of Eden* John Steinbeck relates the plight of the Chinese farmhand Lee. Lee speaks the immigrant's broken pidgin English all his life until one day farmer Samuel discovers by chance that this Chinese boy, who was born in California, can also speak an elegant English. The dumbfounded Samuel takes him to task, asking why in the world he wouldn't speak to the other villagers in normal English. Lee explains that he had in fact made several past attempts to do so, but every time he had been ignored or misunderstood. People just didn't expect English from a Chinaman. 'You see what is,' Lee praises his boss Samuel, 'where most people see what they expect.'

In order to get closer to 'what is', for this book I have chosen the form of a dictionary. China should reveal itself through its terms and its use of them. A second motive was the magic of the characters themselves – their beauty, and their importance to the country.

The written language has played a far stronger cultural role in China than in Europe: it holds the country together. This has been the case since 221 BC when the First Emperor herded the empire's wandering characters into unified squares. The characters were the clamp binding together all the regions of this country that is actually a continent, in whose far corners exist dozens of dialects that have as much or as little relation to each other as English and German. And it has worked for thousands of years: the Chinese owe the intimacy with which they approach their history to their characters, which have scarcely changed over the centuries. Faced with a temple inscription from the 12th century or a stela from the 8th century, a reasonably well-educated Chinese will recognise the engraved characters at once and, with any luck, he will be able to read some of the text. This will bring the Chinese much closer to their own ancient history than we could ever get to ours.

Unfortunately this very peculiarity also has a downside – one that can reduce a student of the Chinese language to despair. Unlike written English,

Chinese characters have absolutely no relation to the pronunciation of the words they represent. Their independent existence as graphic symbols means that they are available to all the various dialects, and that for written Chinese there has never been the need to evolve with the changes in spoken Chinese. They have an air of eternity about them. At the same time it's a burden. If I randomly use some of the 26 letters of the English alphabet to create a hitherto unknown word like 'flimpacoodling', then you will know immediately how it should be pronounced. If the Chinese, however, are confronted with a character they haven't seen before, they are left speechless. In Chinese every word has to be learnt twice: once to know how to pronounce it and a second time to learn how to read and write it. To be able to read the newspaper with any fluency, you need a vocabulary of 3,000–3,500 characters. (The Emperor Kangxi's famous dictionary records more than 47,000 characters, but nobody knows them all. The Ministry of Education did their own calculation: the newspapers and novels of modern China use 99.4 per cent of their ink for the 3,500 most common characters.) So while spoken Chinese is wonderfully simple to learn, reading and writing demand years of swotting. Many an educator in China has wondered whether their schoolchildren's lack of imagination and creativity (although not of intelligence or diligence), can be laid at the door of the rote learning that marks the whole school system.

As well as making learning a drill, Chinese script raises writing to an art form. A scholar's education, emotions and moral sensibility all flow into the characters that are passionately painted or carefully traced with brush and ink. A piece of paper adorned with calligraphy is valued as much as a painting. It is a calling card for whoever held the brush. Chinese characters tell more than their lexical meanings reveal.

This book is not meant to be an encyclopaedia of China, rather it's trying more to be a pocket dictionary. It aims to be as serious and as comic, as absurd and as sad, as enjoyable and as cryptic as China itself is — when you take a closer look. Some things impressed themselves on me over the years, other situations simply thrust themselves upon me, while still others have been devilishly fun to discover. Each entry is a little spotlight, a tile in the mosaic, a bit of a sketch. They can be fitted together as you wish to create a larger picture. And never fear: you don't need to understand Chinese to read this book.

Note

The romanisation in this book follows the official *pinyin* system as used in the People's Republic of China. In the interests of readability, the different tones are not indicated.

At the time of writing the Chinese exchange rate stood at 14 yuan to the pound sterling.

黄 *Huang*

Yellow

If we were to reduce China to a single colour, it would be this one. Mao Zedong may have been the 'Red Sun', but his people remained yellow: yellow is the colour of their skin. The banks of the Yellow River are the cradle of China's civilisation. The Yellow Emperor is their legendary ruler. For other ancient peoples yellow was the colour of the burning sun: not for the Chinese. It is the colour of their earth, the colour of the dust sweeping in from the hostile northern desert. In central China the wind deposits this dust into the loess plateau whose ochre hue dyes the roiling waters of the Yellow River. So it became the colour of fertility, reserved for the emperor – the most potent of all Chinese. This brilliant imperial yellow was woven into his clothing and glazed onto the tiles protecting his palace roofs. It is a proud, noble colour. The Chinese intellectuals who, anticipating the 1989 democracy movement, took a self-critical swipe at the 'yellow culture' did little to change this general perception. To them yellow stood for isolationism and conservatism. They urged the masses to welcome the 'blue culture' of the West which stood for fresh, open waters rather than dusty earth. Such ideas wouldn't stand a chance in today's media: patriotism is a duty, and the Communist Party – that was red the last time you looked – is busy giving itself a new coat of paint. But it's not only the colour of choice for good patriots. Pornography also wears yellow in China. Just look under the 'Yellow Films' section in the battered cardboard box of any well-stocked pirate DVD street trader. Still, no harm's been done to the colour's prestige so far. An internet portal tried to score points with China's yuppies by inventing a 'Generation Yellow'. Cool kids in Shanghai dye their hair a canary yellow. While this is most certainly an attempt at modernisation, it is not necessarily an attempt at Westernisation: the Chinese used to call us Europeans 'Red-headed Barbarians', after crossing paths with a pack of freckled Dutchmen. We later got our own back, calling them the 'Yellow Peril', a lovely example of early intercultural communication.

矛盾 Mao dun

Spear and shield
Land of contradictions

A man was selling shields and spears at the market. 'My shields are the strongest!' he boasted, 'No spear can pierce them.' Later he held up a spear. 'My spears are so sharp, nothing can stop them!' he called out across the square.

'And what happens when someone grabs one of your spears and hurls it at one of your shields?' asked one curious customer. The trader was lost for words. And ever since, the Chinese word for contradiction has been 'spear and shield', *mao dun*.

The descendants of that market seller have long since rediscovered their voice. 'I believe in Karl Marx,' says a young Shanghai business consultant with sincerity. 'That is why I want to give my country as many private businessmen as I can.' China has joined the space age, trumpets the president – 30 million people are still going hungry, reports the premier. China is cool!, brags the scandalous young author from Guangzhou – China breaks my heart, laments the lawyer from Shaanxi.

Some drive BMWs. Others are happy to find a piece of meat in their bowl once a year. 'Communist' China now has a wider gap between its rich and poor than Zimbabwe or India, reports the Chinese Academy of Social Sciences in Beijing.

China confuses. You'll have to be prepared for that. There isn't one China, there are many Chinas. China is the name for a universe with myriad parallel worlds. Some seem never to come into contact with one another, others occasionally brush against each other and sometimes overlap. Still more crash into each other: shield and spear. China is the first world and the third world. You can find yesterday and tomorrow, communist wasteland and capitalist gloss, sexual freedom and a brutal dictatorship, rural poverty and urban gluttony, clever pragmatism and depressing dogma, rapid growth and creeping decay, corruption and heroism. You can find it all – if only you keep your eyes open. Who's to say which of these is the real China?

It isn't easy to figure out what China is, exactly. But perhaps that's a typically European approach. While our thinkers tried to squeeze the awkward world into their ideas and theories, the ancient Chinese tended to honour their ancestors before breakfast, sacrifice to Buddha at lunch-time and pray in a Taoist temple in the evening. Whatever helps. The Chinese didn't worry overly about the hereafter and metaphysics, about dogma and principles. Instead they drew strength from practical life. They let the world go round and let themselves be carried along with it. The Taoists thought man should become one with nature. They were the ones who brought Yin and Yang together in the Tai Chi. They taught their people that you can't have light without dark, or warmth without cold, or the feminine without the masculine, or good without evil – and that both sides are present within each other. Perhaps that's why the Chinese are so relaxed about contradictions: it'll all balance out in the end. And if not – and China was disastrously off-course for long stretches of its history – then at least you haven't wasted your energy on things that you can't control anyway.

'It's because China is a mystery, that it's so dear to me,' wrote the author Zhang Xianliang after spending some 20 years in one of Mao's labour camps, where he nearly died from deplorable conditions and ill treatment. The fact that he became a member of the Communist Party after his ordeal and has remained so ever since, that furthermore his party membership hasn't stopped him from becoming the most success-ful private businessman in Ningxia province or from calling in his essays for a 'rehabilitation of capitalism' – all of this illustrates the Chinese people's endless ability to reconcile the irreconcilable. No one in China would be at all surprised at such a career.

My advice is to beware of anyone who offers a simple explanation for China, whether that person is Chinese or foreign. There just is no explanation for

China, although there is one explanation for any offer of an explanation: lazy thinking. For whatever reason, it seems that people – at least people who have grown up in the West – are not so good at living with contradiction. Put them in a room where utter chaos reigns and they'll leave it with an overwhelming need to reduce everything to a common denominator – supposedly for reasons of logic, but more likely out of a need to create a psychological comfort zone. So people say: China is the future! Or: China is a sinister dictatorship! Well, you can back up both statements with great evidence, but both are about as near to the truth as the blind man who was handed an elephant's tail. 'So that's what an elephant looks like! Round and long like a snake!'

If you ever get hold of China's tail, don't hesitate to keep feeling your way along. You'll be surprised at how much there is to discover. That is the beauty of the country – whether you travel its breadth, lose yourself in its history or let yourself be tossed around in its turbulent present incarnation. Around every corner you can find yourself in new fairy-tale landscapes, glistening with gold here, dripping with blood there.

China is a whole continent: from the tundra in the north to the tropical island of Hainan in the south; from the Taklamakan desert in the west to the economically-booming east coast. You can climb mountains in the Himalayas, travel by camel, sunbathe on tropical beaches and see your reflection in skyscrapers. You'll meet trendy Shanghainese of delicate build and burly, salt-of-the-earth Beijingers. The former will tell you that all Beijingers are country bumpkins and pencil-pushers, squatting in their dusty desert village; the latter will sneer at Shanghai's mollycoddled men and its cosmopolitan women who always manage to work things to their personal advantage. Both Beijingers and Shanghainese will then agree upon the old stereotypes dogging people in other cities. They'll praise the Wenzhouans' entrepreneurial spirit, the Harbinese ability to consume huge quantities of alcohol and the fine palate of the Guanzhou resident. Then they'll warn you that people from Henan are all crooks and thieves, at which the Henaners will be justified in kicking up a fuss. And they all call themselves Chinese.

Just as there is no formula that explains China, there is no truth in talk that the country is an impenetrable, exotic mystery which repels the Western desire for understanding like a water buffalo's skin repels summer rain. As with any culture, so it is with China that the observant outsider can see some things more clearly than the folks tangled up in it. I have rarely met more friendly, welcoming and talkative people than in China, and if anything stands in the way of understanding the country, it is the whirlwind of change that is sweeping through it: nobody is more confused today than the Chinese are about themselves.

It is seldom as rewarding to spend time in a foreign country as it is in China. And it's not only because the lure of its divine culinary experiences will spare any seeker of happiness the detour of Buddha's eightfold path. Nor is it difficult to get to know the Chinese. Europeans and Chinese have much more in common than the Boxer Rebellion. The Chinese are at least as football-mad as we are – no, probably more so. For them, the passion takes on bitter and tragic dimensions. It stands in no relation to their national team's performance, which for more than four decades has shown a masochistic attitude to success. (The Chinese and the goal – they avoid each other.) In China, football and Buddhism share the highest of truths: life equals suffering.

Once you have started walking the path of international understanding, you might be surprised to find that the Chinese share a deep affinity with one particular European nation: the Italians. In fact you might almost be forgiven to think of the Chinese as the Italians of Asia. It starts with their erotic relationship to food and mobile phones, and extends to idolizing their own family, especially their children. And what the Chinese lack in passion and spontaneity, they make up for it with a love of spectacles of all kinds. A friend of mine from Rome spent two years in Hamburg, which is certainly not an ugly town by any definition. Still she suffered terrible homesickness and depression. Yet when she went to chaotic, dirty, frenetic Beijing she blossomed like a lotus flower in a swamp.

差不多 *Cha bu duo*

That'll do

Casual approach to things, which in the English language would often best be represented by a nonchalant 'that'll do'. Tranlated literally, *cha bu duo* means 'lacking by not much' or 'short by just a little' – a conclusion that usually would prod many Europeans to roll up their sleeves for a final spurt. In China, on the other hand, it is generally understood as an exclamation of satisfaction and as such marks the termination of one's efforts. The philosophic basis to that carefree attitude was laid down by the Taoists who advised everyone to unwind and float along with the current of the world whereever that might take you. They took special care to avoid any action interfering with nature and had a profound aversion to perfectionism as to extremes of any kind. As one old saying has it 'What is driven to extreme, must reverse itself; what is coming to full bloom, must decay'. Life according to the *chabuduo*-principle has its gratifications. At the same time it is at least partly responsible for brand-new buildings showing cracks within weeks of completion and foreigners having second thoughts on whether they really should go and see that Chinese dentist. But if we take the Taoists seriously, then Western-style perfectionism is busy fiddling about on its decay. While the Chinese people will continue floating along through world history, curious and amused by it all, knowing their time to bloom is coming … again.

家 *Jia*

The Family
Mr Li, Mrs Wang, Ms Zhang

Scientists from the Chinese Academy of Sciences cal-
culated that China has sufficient space and resources
for around 700 million people. Since neither China's
leaders nor its people have paid too much attention
to their scientists in the past, there are now more
than 1.3 billion Chinese. If you ever feel the need
for company, stand in front of a train station in any
Chinese town and call out loudly, 'Mr Li!' You'll be
in for a surprise. There are more than 105 million
Chinese called Li – almost twice Britain's population.
Some 291 million Chinese share just three surnames:
Li, Wang and Zhang. And once you know the 100
most common names, you can correctly address 1.1

billion Chinese (87 per cent of the population). It's not by chance that the masses are even today called *lao bai xing*: the Hundred Old Names.

The danger of confusion has increased in the last few years. This is not only due to the continuous growth of the population and therefore also of the Li, Wang and Zhang clans, but also to the new fashion in first names. It used to be the custom to choose first names that consisted of two characters. So even today with a little luck you can make the acquaintance of women called 'Intelligent and fragrant', 'Happy and cheerful' or 'Summer-spring'. Names that turn introductions into poetic moments. In recent years, however, it has been considered modern to use first names of just one character, considerably limiting the number of possibilities. The police in the provincial capital of Nanning publicly complained that there are now almost 400 men in their city called Li Jun (Soldier Li), so no one should be surprised if some day they ended up arresting the wrong man. Parents are well aware of the problem too, and often rummage deep in China's trove of historical treasures to name their offspring. The authorities tear their hair when they encounter some of the obscure characters that those well-meaning fathers and mothers have picked. These archaic symbols might be found in long-forgotten works of literature and history, but not in the mainland's modern computer databases. How, if you please, are these names going to be printed correctly on a passport or driver's licence?

For parents-to-be the choice of the right name is an operation whose importance can hardly be overestimated. They plough through bulky tomes in libraries, consult soothsayers and peruse old lunar calendars – all with the aim to find a name that brings as much good luck to the child as possible. There are agencies in China whose sole task is to find company names that will bring success and riches. The right name could put the company back 80,000 yuan. For some tradition-bound families the sight of a new born baby girl was such a disappointment that her parents gave her a name like Zhao di, 'Beckon your little brother', or Lai di, 'Come, little brother', hoping things will work out next time.

If you meet Chinese who introduce themselves as Wang Jiefang, Zhang Jianguo or Li Aijun, then they were probably born soon after the 1949 Revolution. Translated, their names mean Mr 'Liberation Wang', Mr 'Build-the-state Zhang' and Mr 'Love-the-army Li'. Names like these are nothing extraordinary, they sprang from the revolutionary exuberance of the 1950s and 1960s. You can be fairly certain that a 'Resist-the-Americans Wu' (Wu Kangmei) was born at the time of the Korean War (1950–3). Even more ambitious were the parents of the two brothers 'Enlighten-the universe' and 'Conquer-the-universe' Wang, both born in Shanghai at the time of the Cultural Revolution (1966–76). Actually most names in vogue during that special period honoured the new Messiah, Chairman Mao Zedong. One of my friends is the youngest of three children, all born in the 1960s. Their first names are Hong, Wei and Bing. Said one after another, they create the phrase 'Red Guards'. One wonders if their parents knew from the start that they would have just the right number of children?

Today young Chinese find it cool to give themselves an extra English first name, either at school or if they start working for a multinational company. They also use these names amongst themselves, so nowadays Beijing is full of Johns, Tims, Cindys, Peggys and Sunshines. Yes, Sunshine. Many Chinese have translated their love of expressive names into English. Not everyone shows discernment. Perhaps here and there young exchange teachers from the States had a little fun at the expense of their clueless students. In any case, a 'Chloroform Wong' has been spotted in a McDonald's in Hong Kong, I have placed my orders with a 'Typhoon Li' in a Suzhou café and purchased flight tickets on a regular basis from an 'Apple Liu'. A Beijing restaurant owner told me of her friend 'Douchebag Li' and how she once received a job application from a student who preferred to call himself 'Bill Gates'.

As I mentioned earlier, the Chinese put the family name before the first name. Just as Mao Zedong was Comrade Mao and not Comrade Zedong, Hu Jintao the current leader of the Chinese Communist Party is Mr Hu rather than Mr Jintao, which would be news to some newspaper offices. It wouldn't be wrong to interpret this custom as a matter of priorities: the family takes precedence. In the same way, if you ask a Chinese person where he or she is from, many won't tell you their place of birth or where they live, but where their clan is based. A man who was born and brought up in Shanghai can tell you that he's from Shaoxing if his ancestors lived there – even if he has never visited the city. 'Home' and 'family' share the same word in Chinese: *jia*.

Anyone who's seen the old Charlie Chan mysteries knows that Chinese parents have a habit of summoning their offspring with phrases like 'Number Two Son!' This practical, chronological numbering has survived the era of black-and-white movies. Even today in families with a number of children, brothers and sisters dispense with their given names and call out 'Number Four Little Sister!', 'Number Three Big Brother!', or simply 'Old Big One!' The last would be the Number One Brother, taking pride of place in the throng. At birth everyone takes a set place in the family hierarchy, which is recognised in how each is addressed. Over time, this created a clever system of titles that precisely defined everyone's position, while leaving foreigners who had married into the clan mightily confused at family celebrations. No one is just a cousin. For example, we could be talking about your father's brother's son who is older than you (*tang xiong*), or your father's brother's son who is younger than you (*tang di*). Naturally, your mother's brother's son is referred to using a completely different name. Each title clarifies to which generation the person belongs, whether the person belongs to the father's or mother's side of the family, whether he or she has married into the clan or is a blood relative, and where the person fits into the age ranking. Even the wife of the grandfather's elder brother on the father's side (*bo zu mu*) is addressed differently from the wife of the younger brother of the same grandfather (*shu zu mu*).

Behind the complex network of names is the understanding the form of address immediately clarifies who has to show respect to whom, and to what degree. The Confucians, who placed the family at the very centre of Chinese life, were pretty much preoccupied with cracking this old nut: who could order whom about and who had to obey whom. Thus, they believed, family, state – and indeed the world – would keep their proper order. The wife obeys the husband, the younger brother obeys the elder, and the children obey their parents. Particularly this last relationship proven to be rich source of literature and anecdotes over the years. These stories were collected in the *Classic of Filial Piety* and drummed into school-children for centuries. Filial piety (*xiao*) is sometimes translated as 'filial love', but it could just as easily be called 'filial duty'. We hear about the model son who lay down naked at the foot of his parents' bed on a hot summer's night, so that the mosquitoes would enjoy his blood and spare his old folk. Another tale praises the son who, stark naked, used his body heat to melt a hole in a frozen river, so that he could catch a fresh fish for his stepmother, a spiteful old dragon. Also seen as a filial ideal was the grey-haired man who, for the sake of his old mother's delight, dressed up as the baby he once was, down to the rattle in his wrinkled hand. Even well into the late 20th century, schoolchildren in China and Taiwan were encouraged to imitate such behaviour.

In China people have always been expected to use their lives to serve others: sometimes serving the state, generally the family, and always the parents. China's greatest 20th-century writer, Lu Xun, complained about this vicious circle almost 100 years ago: 'Having sacrificed their lives to their parents, and being unable to live independently, our parents now stubbornly demand that their children sacrifice their lives too.' And so it was: each generation devoted itself to the previous one and expected the same from the next one – in the end, no one ever had a life. Traces of this pattern are still seen today, although the old rigid values are disappearing. Economic modernisation has destroyed old family ties and introduced Western-style consumerism and individualism, infecting cities and the youth most quickly. The state's 'one-child' policy was most effective in the cities, and has turned the traditional structure upside-down in many families. Now the whole family is there to serve a single spoiled little brat.

The new China. Once there was nothing more important than the family in this country, and nothing less important than women. Later came the omnipotent state, which did indeed promise women half of the sky, but which still stipulated what it considered correct, proletarian intercourse. Today in Jilin province in northeastern China a law allows the unthinkable: children born out of wedlock. 'Women who prefer to live alone,' states the law, are allowed to have a child with the aid of 'legally accepted medical methods'. In other words: artificial insemination. The law sparked a violent, nationwide debate on the role of the family and the rights of the individual. Even if there's a powerful Family Planning Commission in Beijing, today's citizens are planning their private lives themselves.

So does China have a strict 'one-child' policy or not? Yes and no. As is commonly known in the West, China imposes strict laws and fines on parents who have more than one child. And yet, to the surprise of most Westerners, the one-child family is not the rule, but the exception in China. In fact, only one out of every five children in China is an only child. Why? Because most people slip through the census net. The government grants exemptions to ethnic minority populations or farming families whose first child is a daughter. Some families just don't care about the laws. There exists a huge army of migrant workers that has escaped the controls. (How many of them are there: 100 million? 150 million? No one has really counted the hordes of peasants who have abandoned their ancestors' homelands to work as day labourers in the cities.) Many families pay the fines with little fuss. The fine for an illegal second child is $12,000 in Shanghai. The number of Chinese who can afford that amount is growing daily.

'One baby only, but of better quality!' is one of the many propaganda slogans the Family Planning Commission has plastered on walls in farming villages and factories across the country. In rural areas, where a son is still the only provision for most people in their old age, these slogans have struggled to find acceptance. For that reason the government now allows a second chance for couples who have a daughter. Daughters leave their parents when they marry, becoming part of their husband's family. A son, meanwhile, stays at home and cares for his parents. This longing for sons has led to a dangerous shift in the balance of the sexes, particularly in the countryside. In 2000 for every 100 girls born, 117 boys were born. On Hainan Island it was as many as 130 boys. In a report to the central government, the Population Committee warned that by 2020 there could be 25 million frustrated young men in China unable to find wives. 'One possible result could be an increase in crime and social problems such as forced marriages, the kidnapping of women and prostitution', cautioned the report. The biggest problem today is the ubiquitous ultrasound technology. It is officially illegal to determine the sex of a foetus for the purpose of abortion. However, as with many laws in China, for a little financial contribution this one can also be ignored. Quacks routinely tour villages with mobile ultrasound machines secretly offering their services.

A son is not only considered important for security

in old age. Only male offspring are allowed to make sacrifices to the ancestors and thereby ensure that their souls rest in peace. ('When a son is born / let him sleep on the bed / clothe him with fine clothes / and give him jade to play with,' it says in the *Book of Songs*, believed to be almost 3,000 years old. 'When a daughter is born / let her sleep on the ground / wrap her in common wrappings / and give her broken tiles for playthings.') Immortality in China was normally sought in the eternal continuation of the family line. Mencius (379–289 BC), the most influential disciple of Confucius, said: 'There are three ways to show of lack of filial love. The worst is not to have children.' To be childless was to sin against one's parents.

And so China became the most populous nation on earth.

名片 Ming pian

Visiting cards

People are born twice in China: once into the childbed of their mothers, and once when they have their first business cards printed. Without the cards you are a nobody, or at the most a farmer or a foreigner. The cards are an essential part of the civil servants' and businessmen's uniform, along with that little leather gentleman's bag clamped under their arm and the Richard Clayderman jingle on their mobile phone (the latter being replaced in some cases by the voice of a baby screaming 'Baba! Telephone!'). They are distributed in unimaginable quantities to everyone within reach at every possible occasion. Etiquette demands that the giver presents the card with both hands, holding it between his thumbs and index fingers. Anthropologists explain the phenomenon by the importance of hierarchies in Confucian society: I only know how I have to act, once I know who I'm talking to. Is he above me, below me, or can he go take a running jump? This is why titles are often more important than names. Often you will find half a dozen crammed onto one card.

A few gems from my collection: 1. The card of a provincial school director who had been mentioned in a few foreign newspaper articles. He introduces himself as a 'world famous celebrity' in case his conversation partner has never heard of him. 2. The card of a certain Danba Wangxi from the Tibetan Autonomous Region. It identifies its owner as no less than a 'Living Buddha'. As this Buddha also had five other titles and positions ('Member of the Political Consultative Conference of the Ganzi district' etc), his name and telephone number didn't fit on the card. He scribbled them on a scrap of paper for me before we finished our conversation.

中国 *Zhong guo*

The Middle Kingdom
Self-sufficiency

Probably because they have always been where everyone wants to be – at the centre of the world – the Chinese have never worried too much about orientation. This can be awkward for foreigners. Let's suppose you have lost your way and you ask the old man on the corner for directions. 'Go down to the left,' he says cheerfully and without hesitation. What do you do? That's right, you go ask somebody else. Countless travellers before you have learned the hard way that it is not recommended to go down the street to the left immediately. The rule is: only set off after at least three people have pointed you in the same direction. As the wonderful Chinese saying goes, 'It takes three people to make a tiger.' This refers to a king who said that he would only believe there was a tiger in the city if three people came to him independently to report the beast. Why the need for such caution? Because you will make the astonishing discovery in China that (a) many people are still happy to live their lives without the slightest idea of what the world holds beyond their block, factory or neighbourhood; and that (b) the majority of them would never admit that they didn't know the answer to your question. They would prefer to say 'left' than 'I don't know'. After all, statistics will prove them to be right half of the time. The ignorance about the world beyond the limits of one's own experience is a fascinating phenomenon.

A short while ago a German colleague of mine became friends with a Chinese engineer. His company had sent the engineer to Germany to disassemble an old steelworks, so that it could be shipped back to Shanghai. He invited my colleague to travel around China with him, and my colleague happily accepted. Mr Cheng grew up in Sichuan, but he had worked for seven years in Shanghai and one year in Germany. 'I thought he'd be able to show me around Shanghai, and then be my guide to China,' my colleague said afterwards. It became quickly apparent that Mr Cheng, a friendly, intelligent, educated man in his mid-thirties, could barely find his way around Shanghai. In all the years that he had lived there, he had obviously scarcely left his steelworks. The two of them wandered aimlessly for a few days, but when Mr Cheng managed to buy tickets for the wrong train, my colleague finally took charge of the situation. He had never been to China before and didn't speak a word of Chinese, but with the help of a trusty guidebook he showed his new friend around China. Mr Cheng's biggest surprise came near the end of the trip, as they spent a few days at the foot of the Himalayas, in Yunnan province, thousands of miles from Shanghai. After consulting the map one day, my astonished colleague told his Chinese friend that beyond a range of mountains, a mere half-day's journey away, lay his hometown: Panzhihua in Sichuan. The engineer at first wouldn't believe it. 'You're right!' Mr. Cheng finally exclaimed, and then promptly changed his travel plans. The next day he set off by bus to visit old friends.

Now Cheng is certainly a particularly absent-minded engineer, yet his behaviour is in line with some of my experiences. What doesn't directly affect them isn't of much interest to many Chinese. I should qualify that – this is quickly changing and by now there are a large number of Chinese who know more about Britain or America than the British and Americans know about China. The boundless curiosity and great thirst for knowledge of young people in China is unmistakable. And yet it is relatively new in Chinese society to hear people being praised for exploring unknown territories. Naturally, there were adventurous types in ancient China, but they were always regarded with suspicion. In the Confucian codex, curiosity and a sense of adventure – like bravery and daring – were suspect virtues. Exceptionally, the Taoists agreed with the Confucians on this point: 'Whoever is brave enough to be daring, will die. Whoever is brave enough to be cowardly, will live,' said Lao-tzu.

There was once a famous eunuch and admiral called Zheng He (1371–1434). He was born in the southwestern province of Yunnan into a Muslim family whose surname was Ma (in Chinese that is the first syllable of Muhammad). Troops of the young Ming dynasty (1368–1644) captured the boy, castrated him (he was 13 at the time), and sent him to be a eunuch in the women's quarters of the Ming prince Zhu Di. When his master staged a palace revolt, Zheng He proved a trusty follower and helped the prince seize power. As a reward the new emperor made the loyal Zheng He admiral of his fleet. It was to become the most powerful naval force that the world had ever seen; its size and magnificence would not be surpassed for the next 500 years – not until World War I. Zheng He was the man who brought giraffes to China, and news of China to the land of the giraffes. Between 1405 and 1433 he set out from Nanjing on seven major sea voyages. They took him via Southeast Asia to Ceylon, India, Africa and Arabia. On the first voyage alone 300 ships set sail, carrying 27,870 men. Along with the requisite sailors, there were soldiers, craftsmen, astronomers, pharmacists and meteorologists. They had the compass, invented by the Chinese in the 11th century, to guide them. The flagship was more than 450 feet long; its red silken sails billowed from no less than nine masts and could be seen from a great distance. In comparison, when Columbus set sail from Europe to stumble across the New World in 1492, he commanded only 90 sailors on three cockleshells which – put end to end – were only 200 feet long. On many occasions Zheng He's troops intervened in local conflicts: they killed thousands of pirates, bombarded the city of La-sa near Mogadishu, and declared Ceylon and Malacca – amongst others – to be vassal states of the Ming empire. Yet territorial conquest and trade were not their objectives so much as to spread abroad the word of the power and prestige of the new Ming emperor Yongle.

Under Zheng He China ruled the waves. The empire had better and more advanced ships than Portugal, Spain or Britain. Indeed, in almost every period of China's millennia-spanning history it has been wealthier and more powerful, more populous, more developed and more cosmopolitan than Europe. Even by the beginning of the Tang dynasty at the start of the 7th century, there were 200,000 foreigners living in the city of Guangzhou (also known as Canton): a lively mixture of Malays, Indians, Africans, Turks, Arabs and Persians. And as late as 1820 China's economy accounted, according to the British economic historian Angus Maddison, for almost a third of the total world economy. (By comparison, at the beginning of 2006, China had overtaken Great Britain and France to become the fourth biggest economy in the world – but it still produces just about 6 per cent of global GNP.) The sophisticated design and engineering of Zheng He's fleet would have easily enabled it to circumnavigate the world 100 years before Magellan, and to discover America two years before Columbus. Indeed, the British researcher and former submarine commander Gavin Menzies is convinced that it did just that, and published a book promoting his thesis. You can't blame Menzies. From a European point of view it seems logical to assume that Zheng He launched himself on such an adventure. What is remarkable is this: the Chinese admiral didn't do it. It is fairly certain that Menzies is wrong. There is no evidence in any of the historical descriptions of Zheng He's voyages.

And so the tragic punchline is that the story doesn't serve to illustrate China's greatness, but rather serves as a symbol of what was perhaps the empire's greatest missed opportunity in the last thousand years. Even today the great admiral is scarcely remembered in China. There are more shrines, statues and legends devoted to him in Indonesia and the other southeast Asian lands which he visited than in his homeland. Interestingly, it was only in 2004 that a Chinese government decided to revive his memory. He is finally being celebrated 600 years after his first voyage – and at the same time being used as a propaganda tool. 'The essence of Zheng He's travels to the West is not to be found in the strength of the Chinese navy,' claims Beijing's deputy minister for transport, 'but in China's insistence on peaceful diplomacy while it was a superpower.' Well-chosen words at a time when China is building up its navy; a time when the rise of the country causes the 'Chinese threat' issue to be raised again by conservatives in the United States. Supported by Zheng He's example, a message is to be sent to the world of China's 'peaceful rise'. To guarantee the admiral fits its purpose, the government has cut him to fit: he's celebrated as a sailing Father Christmas who brought neighbouring countries nothing but presents and peace.

The current eulogies are in stark contrast to the way the country formerly dealt with Zheng He's legacy. Right after the death of the admiral and his emperor, something occurred which is incomprehensible to us today: the fleet simply disappeared. The empire cut off its own limb. Four centuries of Chinese seafaring tradition ended at a stroke of an inkbrush. In 1500 the court decreed that anyone building a ship boasting more than two masts would be executed. A quarter of a century later the government had all seaworthy ships destroyed. China had turned its back on the open seas, choosing isolation for its empire. And in doing so it also unwittingly set itself up for an inevitable – if at first unnoticeable – decline, accompanied by humiliation and exploitation at the hands of those who would soon take control of the oceans – the Europeans.

Why did China take this path? Because it was happy in its own self-sufficiency and because, in the wake of Yongle's death, intrigue and power struggles brought Confucian orthodoxy to the fore again. The court scholars' ideals involved the imitation of a distant past; they believed that the barbarians at the edge of the world had nothing to offer the greatest civilisation on earth. China's emperor was their Pole Star, the eternal centre of the heavens around which all the stars of the universe found their place. In their world the traders and merchants who were constantly seeking new wares and new customers were the lowest of the low, far below the good farmers. Only the *xiaoren*, the 'little man' – who was uncultured, common and lacked moral backbone – would strive for profit. So there might be another answer to the question why China chose isolation. China wasn't greedy enough.

Perhaps one can also look at it this way: if you

are standing in the middle of the world, on the axis around which everything else turns, then you don't need to worry too much about north, south, east and west. The points of the compass and left and right are less important than your orientation in a quite different dimension – the vertical one: up and down. What is more necessary is to find your place between heaven and earth, between the people above you and those below you.

麻将 Ma jiang

Mah-jong

The most popular of Chinese games. Also: a highly addictive narcotic. In the West it became known as mah-jong, derived from its pronunciation in southern China. It is played by four people sitting around 144 tiles that are engraved on one side. Its rules are similar to the card game rummy and so it could have ended up as a modest way for bored pensioners to wile away their hours, were it not for:

(a) The fact that it is a game of chance. The Chinese are famously partial to all kinds of gambling.

(b) The noise factor. A conversation overheard in

Beijing : 'Why do the Chinese like mah-jong so much?' Answer: 'Because it's noisy.'

And yet mah-jong was once a card game. Until someone had the idea of carving small tiles out of bamboo and stone, which are great for banging down on the table. Since then the Chinese really enjoyed playing mah-jong. The louder the banging and slamming, the happier the players are, whether they're shuffling the tiles (which in Taiwan is called 'swimming' because of the sweeping arm movements used to 'wash' or scramble the tiles) or in setting them up in front of you ('building the Great Wall'). Hong Kong passed a law awarding compensation to people whose hearing had been damaged at work: the law was created for the benefit of DJs, slaughterhouse workers and employees of mah-jong salons. China's government has been trying for years to re-invent the game as a respectable sport. Yet you still come across articles in Hong Kong newspapers like this one: 'Or Oi-chu was last seen alive eight days ago, playing mah-jong in North Point.' Can you imagine the word 'rummy' in that sentence?

热闹 *Re nao*

Heat and noise
Living on top of one another

China is big, but once you've taken away the deserts and mountains, there is not much space left for so many people to live. It's crowded. People live in tiny flats, fight for scarce university places and at seven in the morning commute to work in buses stuffed with bodies. You would think that these bruised and flattened commuters dream of peace and solitude, of murmuring brooks and exposed peaks. They don't.

Of course there is the odd Taoist hermit hiding in a mountain gorge and the meditating musician in Beijing who claims that, unlike the Europeans, the Chinese seek above all 'peace of the heart'. In the almost 3,000-year-old *Book of Songs*, one passage conjures up a dreamlike, peaceful world, above which 'there were sounds, but there was no chattering'. There is also the famous line by the poet Tang Zixi: 'The mountain was as quiet as the world in its distant past.' Only the mountain isn't there any more. One drizzly day I climbed the Taishan, a revered Taoist mountain in Shandong province. I don't know what it was that irritated me most. Was it the travel guides trumpeting for the whole four hours on megaphones as loud as fire-engine sirens? The screeching of electric saws every 200 yards where workers cut out new steps? (All the holy mountains in China have steps leading from the bottom to their 10,000-foot peaks.) Or was it perhaps the fair at the peak, where three different cable cars disgorged hordes of tourists in front of the souvenir sellers and restaurant touts bickering for business? But there's no need to climb a mountain to experience it. Anyone who has spent a night on the same floor of a hotel as a group of Chinese tourists will know what most Chinese love most is *re nao*: 'heat and noise'. They love to take a plunge into crowds of people already packed together where all hell has broken loose. That's why the paddle boats on the little lake in Beijing's Solidarity Park often become entangled in a watery gridlock every bit as impressive as those on the nearby Third Ring Road; and why people from Hong Kong love to join every queue they find, even without knowing what they are waiting for; and why a restaurant isn't judged by the stylishness of its décor, but by its noise level.

Re nao is a state of being that people strive for because it brings them pleasure and joy. The idea is to dive into as large a mass of people as possible and then, through emitting as many decibels as possible, to reassure each other that you aren't alone in the world. Some people still suspect that encoded in Chinese genes lie the construction plans for fireworks. They invented them and they still use them with a mastery and pizzazz unequalled anywhere else in the world. Today *re nao* is more popular than ever in China, thanks to the increasing number of happy occasions, which historically have been all too rare for this long-suffering people. Under the emperors the peasants struggled to survive. For entertainment they were stuck with private sex and public executions, while the first three decades of Communist Party rule above all brought fear, denunciations and death. In contrast, the ever-present 'heat and noise' today is a very positive sign – on the one hand. On the other hand, the average European seems to be equipped with nerves much more fragile than the average local.

The Chinese draw their strength from *re nao*. Take Xing Weizhou for example, a baseball cap-wearing 77-year-old. Every morning he bounces around in the Sun Altar Park for two hours, kicking a little cloth bag covered with feathers to his friends, mainly women. The game is called *jianzi*. When he's playing with the ladies, he adds a wiry little pirouette between each pass. Xing produces bras ('for the small Chinese breasts'). He has factories all over China and a house in New York. The villa is as big as half of the Sun Altar Park, he says. But he can't stand America, where his children are so busy they don't have any spare time and the neighbours hide in their houses. He spends most of his year in China, in its parks, where he happily leaps and shouts. Just look around, he says beaming, '*Re nao*'.

In any case, America and Europe are funny places. There fishing is a sport that demands patience, concentration, solitude and daybreak. In Beijing things are a little different. Golfing buddies take a Sunday trip into the mountains, where they all line up around a small concrete pool holding their huge sea-fishing rods over the water. Each pool contains roughly double the number of trout thrashing about as anglers standing around it, but seldom more than half a million. Anyone who hasn't caught a fish after five minutes must have been using his golf club by mistake. The fish that have been caught can then be turned over to the pool owner who will grill them on the spot. This is a particular treat because there is a surprising lack of grilled dishes in China's otherwise so inventive cuisine. (Is it perhaps because a barbeque reminds them too much of the campfires of the both feared and despised nomads, of the Mongols' grilled lamb and the Manchus' grilled bear paw? Is grilling for barbarians?) The fish pools shine in a breathtakingly peaceful mountain valley, into which a cool stream gurgles. The treetops rustle in the breeze. The crumbling Great Wall meanders along the top of the ridge. There is only one thing the weekenders from Beijing need to complete their trip: fireworks. And so bangers are soon echoing around the valley, rupturing nature's silence for hours.

Re nao deprivation, by the way, is not to be taken lightly. It can cause health problems in Chinese of a more delicate constitution. I remember receiving a letter from one of my former assistants from Sichuan, who moved to Berlin to write her dissertation. Berlin is very exciting, Ms Yang wrote, there's an overwhelming choice of cultural activities, and whether or not it was a bad omen that she had thrown up right under the Brandenburg Gate on the day of her arrival, she couldn't say. One thing did disturb her though: the silence. For weeks she had been waking up in the middle of the night without knowing why. Until one day she realised that 'it was too quiet. There just wasn't the noise that we always have around us in China. That was unsettling.' And Ms Yang lives right on central Karl Marx Avenue, definitely not a street Berliners would think to praise for its tranquillity.

A real plus about *re nao* is that you don't need to take part in the spectacle, you can just watch (*kan re nao*). The country's cheapest entertainment has always been to watch some hullabaloo or other. Even today the Chinese love to crowd together to see two neighbours bickering or two passers-by fighting. The basic rule is never to get involved, just to quietly enjoy, else you'll be the stupid one. Traffic accidents are considered particularly exciting, they even top watching a foreigner tie his shoelace on the pavement.

The mother of all *re nao*'s was the day of the announcement that Beijing had been chosen to host the Olympic Games. All that night you couldn't understand a word the television reporters were saying because the city was exploding with joy. *Re nao* fits the Olympic spirit: the character re once represented a torch-holder. The opposite of *re nao* is *tai ping*: 'the highest peace'. Here's a tip: *tai ping* can be found in Beijing in only one way. You have to be alone in a swimming pool, with both ears underwater.

运动 *Yun dong*

1. Sport 2. Campaign

Like gunpowder, eating by numbers and most things under the sun except Marmite (Staffordshire, England 1902), Chinese civilisation is credited with inventing fencing, polo and football too. The sports historian Gu Shiquan dates the 'earliest evidence of Chinese sport' as 500,000 years old –quite an achievement considering that *homo sapiens sapiens* has only been around for 40,000 years. Two millennia of Confucian indoctrination have, however, left their mark: whereas mind and soul have always been nurtured, the body seldom was. With the exception of the state organised military-style medal drills, China's citizens leave you with the impression of being a narrow-chested, short-winded people. Older people practice sport preferably in slow motion (see *tai ji quan*, shadow boxing), while many younger people discuss it largely as a high-risk activity. In the run-up to the Olympic Games the government is trying to encourage its people to change this attitude. In Beijing open-air fitness parks appeared overnight. These playgrounds with brightly coloured instruments of torture have been a great success with senior citizens. Among younger people, joining a gym is the latest trend. Yet for most Chinese the first meaning that will spring to mind at the word *yun dong* is still 'political campaign, mass movement'. Mao Zedong loved to initiate such campaigns. Sparrows and rats fell victim to them just as much as 'right-wingers' or 'stinking intellectuals'. Politically-motivated *yun dong* is still popular today in the Party leadership. A recent example is the *yan da* 'Strike Hard' Law and Order Campaign. In March 2004 the Chinese Youth Newspaper quoted the parliamentary delegate Chen Zhonglin as saying that China executes some 10,000 people every year, more than the rest of the world together executes in ten years. (See also: faster, higher, further, Olympic spirit.)

閒 *Xian*

Leisure
A Relaxing Walk Backwards

There is a man walking backwards. Why is he doing this? He follows his heels through the park, in between all the trunks of the trees. He doesn't even look over his shoulder. He steers himself through the gate and walks along the pavement. Cyclists swerve to avoid him. He carries on walking backwards. Why? He stops and with his finger draws a character in the air: *xian*, leisure. 'I'm relaxing,' he says.

In the beginning leisure in China was the moon in a doorframe. A cup of millet wine probably stood beside it, although when the Chinese came to fix the image in the character *xian* they kept quiet about that. Poets though knew the connection, they thrived on it. '... Oh, let a man enjoy his life before it fades and never tip his golden cup empty toward the moon!' These lines of the eccentric genius Li Po are more than 1,200 years old. Drinking and singing about the moon was where the poet found himself, far from the toil and grovelling at the Tang court. According to legend he died in a way that he himself would no doubt have best been able to put into verse. Legend has it that on a boat trip he tried to catch the moon in the waves. The waves then caught him.

The moon in an open door: *xian* is still the word for leisure today. There is a character for the opposite too. 'Being busy' is *mang* 忙 . The character consists of two parts – a heart, and beside it, death.

If there were no more petitions to write or edicts to copy at court, you could well do calligraphy and write poetry. Country folk all the while slaved away, until they were ready to drop dead, or at any rate drop hungrily onto their straw mats. But life granted them, too, some gifts: the moon and liquor. When the fields lay fallow people sought comfort in these two things. Come autumn the farmers too would sing to the moon and carouse. They had many days ahead of them when they wouldn't need to work the fields. To this day you can stumble across villages in China without an ounce of meat to dish up – but a village without liquor you will never find.

Zhao Ziyang, the Communist Party's former general secretary, visited a peasant village in the poor Shaanxi province in the 1980s, a friend recounted. Zhao asked the farmers what they did in their free time? Free time? they replied, stumped. Zhao rephrased his question: in the evening, after work, what do you do then? In my friend's anecdote, one farmer scratches his head and finally replies without any embarrassment: we screw. And then? Then we rest, the farmer said. He tugged on his beard, and thought some more: and then we do it again. You see, said my friend, that's why there are 1.3 billion Chinese.

There is no lack of evidence proving the Chinese are more than our match. For example in the construction of space rockets or in the ability to fall into a deep sleep at any time, as if by command. (I recently saw a picture of a man in Beijing who had skilfully turned one of those thick entrance-blocking cordons in a park into his own personal hammock.) They show particular aptitude in the art of squatting (*dun*). Contemplative sitting in general plays an important role in life in China, and squatting is what you do when you don't have a seat available. What's that? You think you can squat too? That's a lot like the crow who puffed out its chest and screeched at the nightingale, 'I can sing too!'

The Chinese have become masters at parking their bums on the lower part of their legs. So they are able to settle into contemplative squatting in the most surprising of places. You see them happily slurping away at melons, taking photos and reading newspapers as they squat on pavements, at bus stops and in waiting rooms. It is a mystery to me how they manage to lay the whole of their soles flat to the ground and hold this position. Untrained foreigners who attempt to imitate this gymnastic achievement, will fall over in seconds and simply roll down the street. The Chinese, on the other hand, who absorb the ability to squat through their mother's milk, often prefer it to simple sitting. If a bench is available they use it – to squat on and smoke a cigarette. After all, the view is better from up there.

I used to see it as the characteristic pose of a people that has always had to wait for everything, and wasn't given much space in which to wait. But there is more to it. Squatting is not always voluntary. Authority figures like to command a group of underlings to squat before them. This helps them to keep control of the situation – and to elevate themselves. Officers do it to their soldiers, head teachers do it to their pupils, and once at the Guangzhou train station the security staff did it to us: they forced everyone waiting for trains to squat. We were separated according to the trains we were waiting for and had to squat on the square in front of the station. (In contrast to simply sprawling on the ground, squatting requires less space and leaves less energy for misbehaving.) As I said, I fell over straight away. Chinese friends give a rather more banal reason for their propensity for squatting: the pit toilet, the long drop. Certainly the association of toilet and squatting is so natural to many Chinese that in aeroplanes you will sometimes find shoe prints on the toilet seat.

In 1994 the government gave workers a second day off each week. Since then the Chinese too have enjoyed having Saturday and Sunday off – at least those workers who are employed by the state or foreign companies. Never has there been as much free time in China's cities as today.

Nor has there been as much money. People drive cars. They travel. Some pay thousands of yuan for the permission to rip the side out of an innocent hill with one of the People's Liberation Army's big guns. Budding entrepreneurs get drunk in bars listening to cover bands play John Denver or Kurt Cobain. The *nouveau riche* hire the company of film starlets. Politicians and CEOs let themselves be invited into dark clubs where a bottle of cognac will put you back £150.

'In the United States people go to the supermarket and to church in their free time,' says Victor Yuan of the market research organisation Horizon. 'In China people prefer karaoke to the supermarket.' Karaoke is actually a Japanese invention, but it has long evolved beyond a fleeting mainland fad. Massage and more cost extra. People don't only do karaoke to chirp new Wang Fei songs and Mao's old hymns. Men go there to find *xiao jie* – young ladies – who in turn go because there is no easier way for a girl to get rich quick in this country. 'There are three new classes of aristocrats in China,' a famous propaganda recording star once told me. 'The *nouveau riche*, the political cadre and the prostitute.' At the time we were sitting in a bordello disguised as a tea house in the old imperial city of Xi'an that went by the name 'Blue Jasmine'. The owner was the local police chief's brother. Where did the girls come from, I asked, pointing at the garishly made-up ladies who sat on a bench in the corner, like chickens on their roost. Our host stared at me. 'What girls?' he asked. Now it was my turn to stare at him. Some people in China don't do anything for fun. They want above all to be different from others – and better – and then have the power to show it off. These are the people who endure the expensive

70

Anne-Sophie Mutter guest appearance in Beijing just to be able to tell at least three different friends on their mobile phones about the luxury they have treated themselves to – while the show is still going on, of course. The leisure researcher Yuan believes that as today's China nervously sets off in new directions, many people just appear to be enjoying their lives, but only one group really is: the elderly. They barely have any money but it is enough to pay for the monthly pass in the Earth Altar Park. That has always cost just three yuan, 20 pence.

Every morning you can see them in high spirits, dancing the tango and waltzes around the altar – in wellies if it is raining. Neighbours escape their stuffy, tiny flats and meet there under the shady elms for a game of mah-jong. Every morning in the summer you will find the 78-year-old former masseur Meng doing his 40 press-ups without a shirt on. 'As long as you have enough to eat and warm clothes to wear, everything's just fine,' says Meng. With those basics he is ready for the day, for *wan*: pleasure. Meng grins. *Wan* actually means 'playing', but it can be used for everything that is fun. If someone says 'let's play together this weekend' it can mean everything from an innocuous visit to a park where hedges have been trimmed to look like brontosaurs to a much more consequential romantic discussion of those hedges. You can 'play' a man, a woman, drugs, shares or tennis. (A friend of mine learnt the hard way that the Chinese play differently to us. Working for a small company in Taipei, he was trying to convert the Taiwanese to board games. 'Not easy,' he sighed in his e-mail. 'When you say "play" the first thing the Chinese think of is eating and drinking. Food is also what they think about if you mention "having fun", or "leisure", or whatever … ')

In a newly-developed area beyond Beijing's Fourth Ring Road, the diggers missed a few fields. Open land, kites flying, an old shed, a tree stump, and an 80-year-old woman who sits down groaning. 'We've just started learning,' she pants, pointing at a group of people who have formed a circle, holding their fans in their right hand, a colourful cloth in their left. They are dancing the *yang ge*, an old country dance that the communists on their Long March towards the revolution observed in villages of the loess plains. They loaded it up with ideological baggage and brought it down to the cities. The dance has outlived the ideology and you can see mostly old people dancing it mornings and evenings – under bridges, at crossroads and in car parks. Most of the dancers are women, sometimes a few old men stand there too, tooting on instruments and banging out the beat.

Here on this scarred field though, a 70-year-old man is whirling about, his baggy shorts flapping against his bony frame. He breaks out of the circle and dances around the new onlooker, cock of the walk. He crows, 'The Communist Party lets us party.' He doesn't say it, or shout it, he sings it, improvising verses in the theatrical singsong style of Beijing opera. 'Things are getting better every day,' he sings as he clowns around. 'Space ships fly through outer space.' Swish – the fan slices through the air like a sword. 'Power comes from the barrel of a gun.' He is giggling now. The grey harlequin continues to jump around. 'Important for our health,' he croaks, drawing the vocals up and down the octaves, 'Im-por-or-tant, that our grea-eat fa-atherland is he-ealthy.' The graceful old ladies are absorbed in their dance, their hips swaying.

China is a country where even the national sport, eating, serves a higher purpose: namely to supply the body with the medically correct doses of yin and yang, hot and cold, sweet and bitter. Nor is the act of playing committed for its own hedonistic end. Hobby, what do you mean hobby? grumbles a kite-flyer on the edge of town. He must be in his mid-sixties. 'I do it for my eyes and neck muscles. Can you imagine how much effort it is to be looking up all the time?' That is why you see men and women walking rather strangely through Beijing, Shanghai and Guangzhou – against the flow of people and traffic. They are using forgotten muscles. They think it is healthy to walk backwards through China's cities – adventurers, every one of them.

Men with long brushes also walk backwards through the Earth Temple Park. They are street calligraphers and give the poems of the Tang and Song dynasty a fleeting form on slabs of the pavement. They use water as ink, and the stone is their paper. 'If you only walk forwards,' says the retired teacher Wang Jiuxiang, 'you only train one part of your brain.' Wang invented the giant outdoor brush about 10 years ago, by cutting a sponge to size and wedging it in a long plastic handle. A clip regulates the water reaching the sponge's tip. And so teacher Wang brought calligraphy out of the artist's workshop and onto the streets. He also banished many hobby-calligraphers' worries about expensive rice paper, which they had used at home. 'Four characters and you've filled up a page and spent another yuan. That makes you nervous,' says Wang. Pensions aren't generous and calligraphers, above all, seek tranquillity. Their creations are ephemeral, lasting no more than three or four minutes, but that doesn't bother them. They are spending time with their friends. Passers-by admire and comment on particularly spectacular verses – for example, those by Li, a retired bookkeeper. Li Wendao imitates Chairman Mao Zedong's calligraphy. 'A great leader,' says Li, 'and an accomplished calligrapher and poet.' In one respect Li surpasses the Great Chairman himself: he writes Mao's verses backwards.

Sometimes in winter a small miracle occurs. Teacher Wang adds a little salt to the water. The characters freeze and the verses are like little sculptures, fixed in a silvery frost. Wang fiddles with the clip and from his brush flow the verses of the drowned poet Li Po. He writes in powerful, clear *kai shu* (block characters):

'... Oh, let a man enjoy his life before it fades'

'Can you imagine that? Silver frost?' Wang asks excitedly.

炒 Chao

Frying

1. Also called pan stirring. The most important of China's frying techniques. You toss the sliced ingredients into the heated wok and quickly stir them around. The somersaulting bits of food take on the flavour of the marinade, as tongues of flame lick them from the open fire heating the wok. The technique cooks the dishes extremely quickly. The resulting taste and consistency are in no way comparable with what Western frying produces, where meat and vegetables are more or less abandoned to their fate.

2. A technique borrowed by marketing and political circles, whereby a dry old topic is cooked up into a

hype. Dull books can be 'fried', as can insipid pop stars or Palaeocene party congresses. The result is rarely fresh or easily digestible; more often it is a con aimed at the general public.

See also *xuan chuan*: propaganda.

吃 *Chi*

Eating
Healthy, happy and full

'Then God's temple in heaven was opened, and there came flashes of lightning, rumblings, peals of thunder, an earthquake and a great hailstorm.' So it is told in the Book of Revelation, and while theologians still argue about how the vision of the apocalypse was imparted to the Apostle John, to me it doesn't seem improbable that the holy wrath was revealed to him during a visit to one of Europe's Chinese restaurants.

You don't agree? And yet surely you aren't one of those people who have read a few books on Buddhism and now think that they know the truth of things? Zen Buddhists state that a book about enlightenment relates to enlightenment no more than a finger pointing to the moon relates to the moon. Clever discussions about nirvana have as much to do with nirvana as a colourful menu has to do with the food it presents. Who would think of spreading butter on the menu's paper, however pretty and well designed? And as far as the cooking in European Chinese restaurants goes, it certainly leans nearer to the printed menu card rather than the food end of the spectrum.

In Buddhism whoever wants to be granted enlightenment, must set out on that journey himself. No priest or monk can help. It is no different with food. If you want to know what a spring roll is, take a bite. And by that I mean a bite of a real Chinese spring roll, from Shanghai, Beijing or Guangzhou, not the indefinable biomass plumped on a plate in a Chinese restaurant in Europe. Astonishingly, these restaurants remain popular. People believe they can go for a 'Chinese' and by the time their bill comes, they are qualified to pronounce judgement on Chinese cuisine. I often wondered how to make it clear to Europeans what a dull imitation they are being served, until one day I realised something: the exact same swindle is perpetrated on the other side of the globe. While in Guangzhou recently I made myself comfortable at the 'Rose Garden' restaurant along a picturesque riverbank. The restaurant advertises itself as 'Western', and I ordered their 'Omelette with Bread'. I was brought a ketchup dumpling wrapped in egg served with two triangular sandwiches garnished with a sprig of coriander and half a cocktail cherry. The slices of bread were so securely glued together with peanut butter that nothing could have pulled them apart, and they were as thin as if the fat Laughing Buddha (the one boasting the mighty stomach on which little children sometimes play) had been sitting on them, using them as his personal meditation mats. The omelette and the bread were served with a spoon. There was plenty to eat, and plenty to digest.

The Chinese have invented a category of food that doesn't exist anywhere else in the world – *xican*, 'Western food'. This food is very like 'Chinese food' in Europe. It is a construct, a postcard created at the point of consumption, showing a foreign universe and its Milky Way, suns, planets and comets all squeezed onto one five-by-three-inch rectangle. And there the universe lies: in the wrong colours and crumpled. A starting point for your dreams, nothing more. Both the British going to get a 'Chinese' and the Chinese going to get a 'Western' are enticed by the foreignness, by the chance to escape from what they usually eat. They are flirting with being cosmopolitan. In China there is a prestige factor too: the West is modern, it stands for progress and the future. It is trendy.

Western food is expensive in China. The result for Chinese diners is even greater disappointment with the food they are served. How poor it seems in comparison to their own cuisine! This is what people in rich countries feed themselves? Poor them. 'Now and then we go to a Western restaurant,' a designer of cigarette lighters in the southern Chinese city of Wenzhou tells me proudly. (The guy has become something of a minor celebrity here for designing a lighter shaped like a toilet seat.) But then he bends nearer, 'Honestly though: I don't like the stuff.' The menu in the restaurant he occasionally visits, the ambitiously named Paris Louvre, largely depends on variations of one dish: steak with fried egg. 'I always eat three portions,' our rather portly acquaintance tells us, 'and I'm still not full.' And that dry, crumbly thing that we eat in the West, 'that bread stuff', he says with a pitying look at me, 'I really cannot stomach.'

Generally no distinctions are made – not between French, Spanish, Greek, British or Italian food, certainly not between Tuscan, Sicilian and Umbrian cuisine, just as the average European is not going to differentiate between the food from Shanghai, Guizhou, Manchuria, Sichuan and Guangzhou. We will quite happily chuck into one frying pan the simpler Beijing fare and the sophisticated Hangzhou cuisine, Shandong's dumplings and Hong Kong's dim sum, sweet and sour food from Hunan and the natural, unadulterated food of Chaozhou. We'll top it off with Chongqing's volcanic hot sauces and a helping of sweet Zhejiang flavours, add a spoonful of starch, stir once and call it 'Chinese food'. Delicious.

Perhaps this is the moment to add a few words

about old China's torturers – inventive chaps. The worst punishment was death 'by a thousand cuts'. The name itself is an understatement. At the beginning of the Ming era (1368–1644) dexterous executioners had raised the number of cuts to no less than 3,357. The condemned man would have his flesh cut from his bones in thin slices over a period of three days. He had to be kept alive all this time. 'At every tenth cut the executioner announces the current total,' a report from 1510 tells us. 'Starting at his chest, Liu was given 35 cuts on the first day of execution, each one no bigger than a thumbnail. He bled a little at the first cuts, but then the blood flow stopped. It is said that a condemned man can go into such an extreme shock that all his blood withdraws to his loins and thighs, only gushing out when the chest is opened up.' There was also a master executioner who laid his criminals above a bed of freshly planted bamboo plants. With the right sort of bamboo and warm, humid weather, the seedlings could shoot up more than a foot overnight, easily enough to run the victim through. On the whole though, the torturers copied their ideas from chefs, who had long known a wide variety of interesting ways to prepare fresh meat. If the punishment was *gua*, the man was cut into thin strips. *Bo pi* meant he would be skinned and thrown in the wok. For *hai* the condemned man was turned into mincemeat. Even today Chinese food abroad has this affinity to bodily abuse. Only today it is the chefs who are inspired by the torturers. The victim is no longer laid above bamboo, he is served it – generally fresh from the tin, with the slightly acidic taste of urine that the bamboo has taken on in a rusty ship's hold somewhere between Shanghai and Liverpool.

The first evidence of a link between cooking and human rights abuses can be found 3,000 years ago, when the Zhou dynasty rulers threw rebellious officials into a great big *ding* and let them stew. The *ding* is a beautiful, massive bronze pot that stands on three feet and is used to braise meat dishes. In the Zhou era it became the highest symbol of lordly dignity and power. The highest official in the Zhou court was the chancellor; his Chinese title *jiazai* originally meant 'Chef'. The ministers below him all had titles like 'Lord of Salt' or 'Lord of Gruel'. Historians trace this merging of political and culinary vocabulary back to China's tradition of making sacrifices to their ancestors. The sacrifice basically was a ritualised conversation in which one sought protection and prosperity from one's dead forefathers. It was the most important function of the kings and princes. Essentially, a sacrifice was a magnificent banquet, with incredible amounts of warmed wine, steamed fish, braised meat and fried vegetables. The spirits of the dead could feast on it first, and then the court devoured what was left. This belief in 'hungry spirits' whose bellies regularly need filling has survived in Taiwan, Hong Kong and in rural areas of China up to the present day.

This may well be the source of the Chinese people's religious devotion to gourmet cuisine. How else can you explain the miracle of the world's finest and most varied cuisine being created in the midst of an endless stream of natural catastrophes and famines? There are half a dozen different techniques and words alone for what we in English call 'braising'. No wonder the

Chinese grow up believing that 'stomach and heart can't be separated' (*xin fu bu fen*). The Chinese have 'have been exhorted for at least the past 20 centuries to reflect about what they eat, and to understand what food means for their bodies and their wellbeing,' writes the French historian Françoise Sabban in her foreword to *Food in China*. 'Let us admit that we have some catching up to do.' And that from a Frenchwoman.

Indeed, real Chinese food is not just filling. At the very least is also good for your health, and ideally, it makes you happy. So don't be surprised at the pages devoted to it herein. Nothing is as important in this country. Eating is to the Chinese what sex is to the Europeans – only it is celebrated and practised even more obsessively. No one would greet you in Europe along the lines of 'Screwed yet today?', but in China it is absolutely normal to say hi with an 'Eaten yet today?' The Chinese confront the world with their mouths. We count 'heads', the Chinese count 'mouths' (*kou*); their term for 'population' is *ren kou*: people's mouths. An open mouth is often a sign of fear or shock to Europeans, for the Chinese it might have been the only part of the body through which they got something good out of this world. Admittedly, that isn't always so. If you suffer, you 'eat bitterness' (*chi ku*); if you are jealous, you have 'eaten vinegar' (*chi cu*). Yet China has always found comfort and bliss in the kitchen, which is why food is 'the people's heaven' as an old saying has it. It is the centre of life, the reason for being. For the Americans food is just fuel to get them through the week, noted the US-based Chinese historian Sun Longji. 'The Chinese give the impression though, that they live in order to eat.'

Thank God, a neutral European might add. It has made Beijing a land of milk and honey for me and for all the foreigners who live here. The Feiteng Yuxiang, for example, serves the capital's best *shui zhu yu* – 'water boiled fish' – which is a very misleading description of a dish that transforms tender slices of filleted fish into dynamite. The fish is served in a massive metal dish of highly spiced oil that is carried to the table by the strongest waitresses, bubbling and hissing all the while. Just looking at it is quite a shock for the first timer. The sight of it alone gets your adrenaline pumping. Your eyes can make out nothing at first but spitting, seething lava – a mountain of chilli peppers that the waitress carefully ladles from the fish pot for several minutes. The waiting whets your appetite even more and can drive you crazy with anticipation. Then finally your first bite – the hit you have been waiting for. Barely have we opened the door of the 'Home of the Bubbling Fish' (as the restaurant's name would be translated into English) – and all the dirt, noise and traffic of this once great city, that has now sold its soul to a third-class idea of modernity, washes off us. Instead we rub our eyes with surprise, and our stomachs with glee – for as long as we still can: we can barely see out of the slits of our eyes any more, our cheeks are becoming chubby, and we have lost sight of our belly buttons ages ago, what with rounding out of the abdomen. And when we Chinese and for-eigners get sentimental together, we simply plop a piece of spring bamboo into each other's mouths and then drink with coarse oaths and tender verses to old splendours and new adventures. In the end we're all embracing each other and the world outside has disappeared, as if by magic.

It is quite normal for people to queue for an hour for such a meal. In the 'Bubbling Fish' the waitresses direct the storm of customers with megaphones and electronic display screens. You can't order in advance. In Taiwan, where you will find certain Chinese characteristics in an even more concentrated form, the wedding banquet itself has replaced the bridal couple as a wedding's main attraction. The last time I was in Taipei I was a guest at the wedding of a musical couple. He was the singer in a death metal band, she played the bass guitar. They normally perform with black and white make-up on their faces. Here they stepped into the darkened ballroom of a luxury hotel accompanied by classical music. He was in a suit, she in a white bridal dress, and both carried a candle. It was very romantic, but nothing compared to the *shang cai xiu*, the 'food serving show' that the compère announced as soon as he had shooed the couple off stage. 'Children, don't be scared,' we heard him say just before the lights went out. A drum roll and bombastic music then made us all start. You would have thought Mike Tyson was about to enter the room, or at the very least the state president. What did come was ... a lobster on a dish. Or rather, at first torch-bearers marched in from both sides of the room and swept round the 350 guests in a carefully planned choreography, before finally crossing torches. At this point flame-throwers on the stage sent fire spurting towards the roof to announce the evening's climax: the entrance of the aforementioned lobster, braised in cognac, carried triumphantly down the centre aisle between the tables by the head chef himself. The applause as the chef and lobster climbed onto the stage was deafening. There is quite a competition amongst hotels in Taiwan to offer the most impressive *shang cai xiu*.

I was not surprised at the results of a survey in Chongqing. The survey announced this Yangtse city's highest earners: it was the chefs. In 2004 a chef there could earn 12,000 yuan per month – three times as much as the highest earners in the IT industry (4,500 yuan) and more than most Chongqing factory directors and managers (up to 10,000 yuan). In contrast, waiters earn as little as 400 yuan per month. I have only once met a Chinese who despaired at his people's fixation with food. His name was Jack and he was a steelworks engineer from spicy Sichuan. 'The Chinese waste too much time and energy on food,' he sighed. 'If they would spend half that time on scientific work, then perhaps our country would finally make some progress.' Shaking his head resignedly, he spooned his rice noodles from his bowl.

It is said that Confucius never touched a dish if the cook had committed the *faux pas* of putting the wrong sauce on the meat. To the ancient Chinese, salted dried meat just cried out for fish sauce, while the cooked juices of ant larvae were a must with spicy dried meat. The Confucian classic, *The Rites of Zhou*, reports that of the 4,000 servants in the court of the western Zhou (11th century to 770 BC), a total of 2,271 worked in the kitchens and wine cellars. Apparently 342 people were solely devoted to preparing fish. We have hard proof that these numbers were surpassed 2,500 years later in the Ming emperor Wanli's ministry of food. Yet such excess was obviously not pleasing to the heavens. Not soon after the Manchus overran the country, ending the Ming dynasty (1368–1644). The Manchus were a horse-riding people from the north. Their emperors took on the dynastic name of Qing (1644–1911). So it was actually foreigners who ruled as China's last dynasty. And wasn't the Mings' downfall their own fault? As much as they loved good food, the Confucians had always warned that every good thing should be enjoyed in moderation. An emperor who gets carried away is inviting decadence and corruption. He is gambling with the Mandate of Heaven.

On the other hand, it was always the food that made the Chinese Chinese and distinguished them from the non-agrarian barbarians – people who ate raw food and people who didn't eat cereals were obviously barbarians. Naturally that referred above all to the nomadic peoples in the north, whose awesome presence had caused the Chinese to build the Great Wall. Why did they even think the Wall was necessary? The example of the Manchus shows that the Chinese theory of their cultural supremacy had a catch: the barbarians, which by definition had to be inferior to Chinese civilisation, had in fact always been the greatest danger to it. However, the Chinese people's pride in their own food and their belief in its power were so strong that during the Han dynasty the government official Jia Yi (200–168 BC) went so far as to suggest that the attacking Huns could be tamed with food. Instead of building more barracks, Chinese restaurants should be opened on the border. Jia Yi was convinced that 'If the Huns acquire our tastes, taking a liking to our boiled rice, our stews, our fried fish and our wine, then they will be decisively weakened.' In my case, 2,200 years later, these tactics certainly worked.

How can you tell where refinement ends and decadence begins? I once stayed in the little town of Qufu to meet some descendents of Confucius. The Kong family is a clan that today numbers more than four million people, scattered around China and the world. Norway's population is no larger. (Kong was Confucius's family name. Some people respectfully called him *Kong fu zi*, Master Kong. It was the Jesuits, who were sent to Beijing by the Pope in the 17th century, who then referred to the great man as 'Confucius'.) In the Kongs' ancient family palace I was proudly told that there had been a servant family working for the clan that for generations had no other task than to clean and cut bean sprouts. Nothing unusual in the houses of the nobility, it seems. Yet the overwhelming majority of the people were farmers. For most of the year they were happy with cabbage stalks and some soya sauce, so that they didn't have to choke on dry rice and noodles. This left it largely up to the aristocracy and the rich merchants to create a more sophisticated Chinese cuisine. There are reports of taverns that could seat over 1,000 people as early as the Song era (1279–960 BC). There, traders and manual workers feasted on sautéd mussels, steamed liver with lychee, and the twice-cooked purple suzhou fish – thus planting the seeds of gourmet cooking that would later flourish among the general public. Even then, menus boasting more than 230 dishes were nothing unusual in tea houses and restaurants in

Kaifeng and Hangzhou. At that time Hangzhou was the greatest city in the world. There were probably one million people living there in the 13th century. In comparison, Venice – Europe's pride and Marco Polo's home town – seemed provincial with its 140,000 inhabitants.

The South's culinary arrogance towards the North probably dates from that period. Northern China is cursed with poorer soil, a harsher climate and regular droughts. If you ask the spoilt southern Chinese what the North has contributed to their country's rich culinary traditions, they will admit little more than noodles, cornbread rolls and garlic. Some northern Chinese get their own back, suggesting that precisely because the southern Chinese have been blessed with the mild, warm and fertile part of China, and because their food drops right into their mouths, they are rather unimaginative folk. 'They have practically no variation in their seasons, so they eat the same food all year round. That makes the southerners pretty simple,' the writer Liu Zhen claims to have observed. 'On the other hand, nature has made us northerners a much more adventuresome bunch.' Liu Zhen comes from Shandong, a province known above all for its *jiao zi*, dumplings that the locals like to eat while munching on a raw clove of garlic. However, she lives in Shanghai where she underwent a long and passionate training to acquire a gourmet's tastes. It was with her that I first ate deep-fried water-snakes.

Today, as in the past, it is often *nouveau riche* businesspeople and power-drunk officials who cross the border between ingenuity and crassness. A few years ago, for example, one trend that swept southern China was to sprinkle gold dust on food. Later, a stir was caused by reports of a restaurant in Changsha that supposedly used the breast milk of pregnant farm girls to prepare particularly nutritious dishes. The story of 12 Hong Kongers who spent 360,000 yuan for an evening meal in a Xi'an restaurant also hit the news. The tea alone came to 10,000 yuan, the owner revealed.

Such anecdotes though shouldn't divert us from the truth that the essence of Chinese cooking is not to be found in its excesses. Yuan Mei (1716–98) was a scholar who became something of a celebrity foodie in the Qing era. His *Sui Garden Menu* is an entertainingly told cookbook, interweaving 300 recipes and a list of famous teas and wines with tips and warnings to serious lovers of good food. It is said that Yuan Mei was once invited to a meal at the house of a rich merchant where the table bent under the weight of over three dozen exquisite dishes. After the meal he went home and the first thing he did was to cook a simple bowl of rice, 'to fill a little hole'. His equally famous countryman Li Yu had the dew from bamboo leaves and roses collected, so that he could drizzle it over steamed rice. China's greatest gourmets looked for refinement in simplicity. They praised the things that were by nature good. The same holds true today in Chinese cooking: fresh, quality ingredients are a must. This is why many Chinese still find it essential to go to the market every day. Even in that capital of global finance Hong Kong, frozen meat doesn't stand a chance. The chicken still has to be kicking upon purchase. (After a number of global bird flu alarms, this habit is driving virologists around the world crazy. The markets in southern China are suspected of breeding and harbouring the viruses.)

The best cooks know how to tease out the essence of the ingredients. They strengthen the flavours with a light touch, using harmonious complementary ingredients and clever contrasts. This is why, all High Wycombe's Chinese dishes from A1 to Z173 should go straight into a composting bin.

筷子 *Kuai zi*

Chopsticks

1. Culinary implement. Used to bridge the gap between plate and mouth; can also be used in various operations in the kitchen, as well as on, beside, and below the dining table. Chopsticks are the Chinese equivalent of the Swiss army knife. They can be used to scrape out bottles, to open mussels, to turn fish and to spear slippery pieces of tofu as well as nasty kung fu opponents (see Jackie Chan).

2. Instrument for measuring a foreigner's ability to integrate: 'Great! You can eat with chopsticks!' (see *zhong guo tong*, old China hand).

Found most often in the modern world in disposable form. The active lifespan of the average chopstick today can be measured in minutes. Disposable sticks have thoroughly taken over, whether in good restaurants, school canteens or dirty noodle stands on the streets. Criticism of this practice is now growing. Regular sandstorms and catastrophic floods have made the protection of the forests a major theme in China. With 1.3 billion Chinese throwing away their chopsticks after every meal, many trees are in a tight spot. According to the government, China produces 45 billion pairs of chopsticks every year, sacrificing 25 million trees to fast food at the same time. Beijing Forestry University was the first to take the logical step of banning disposable chopsticks in its canteen. (Chinese environmentalists are not only worried about habits in the kitchen. Now they are also turning their attention to the bathroom as the *People's Daily* reports: 'China, the land credited with inventing toilet paper, also uses too much of it – demand for it is putting pressure on our valuable wood resources.')

The Chinese have been eating with chopsticks

for 3,000 years; only for soup or sauce do they use a spoon. Chopsticks are part of their cultural heritage. You can use them for folk dances, fortune-telling and even quick personality tests – old books can tell you that people who hold their chopsticks with three fingers are down-to-earth folk, while those who use all five fingers are destined for great things. Foreigners happy to finally have managed to help themselves to some roasted peanuts without breaking more than two fingers, should contain their jubilation. The real test lies elsewhere. If you have the ambition, turn to a dish of slippery *cao gu* (straw mushrooms). I would recommend that you try this exercise with no-one else sitting next to you, unless you are at your little child's birthday party. Afterwards perfect your technique on a bowl of wobbly tofu and finally show off your mastery with thick, long, home-made noodles coiled in an oily soup. We can compare notes when you come back from the dry cleaners.

The emperors and high officials favoured silver chopsticks as these were said to change colour if they touched poisoned food. In the Qing dynasty, ivory was also fashionable. Over the past millennia there is, in fact, scarcely a material that has not already been used to make or coat chopsticks – lacquer, gold, jade, porcelain, sandalwood and rhinoceros horn, to name but a few. The 'hundred old families' stuck to bamboo or wood. Disposable sticks only conquered the People's Republic in the 1990s, arriving from Japan and Taiwan. For a long time the government encouraged the trend for reasons of hygiene. If chopsticks are to be disposable, some say, then at least produce them from sustainable bamboo, which grows back quickly. The melancholy fate of bamboo sticks was sung by the Ming poet Cheng Lianggui long before the throw-away era: 'Toiling chopsticks of bamboo be the first to taste the sweet and sour that others then savour as you wander in vain back and forth.'

阴阳 *Yin yang*

Yin and yang
The Tao in the kitchen

A Chinese (C) and a foreigner (F) meet. F is inquisitive, perhaps also a little hungry, C only wants to be polite:

C: You must come for a meal!
F: But I wouldn't want to be any trouble –
C: Not at all! You are most welcome.
F: No, I couldn't –
C: You must, you must! –
F: No, really, no, I couldn't!
C: Yes, yes. You must, I insist!
F (happily): All right then, if you insist!
C (thinks): Good Lord!

Chinese table etiquette has only a few rules. One of them is: do not take every invitation seriously. Pingpong dialogues like the one above are not rare, but according to the cultural script they usually end with a noncommittal 'Another time!' Between friends invitations are, of course, actually to be understood as such, but even then the invited person may suspect that his visit will be used to ask a favour from him. Nor is this in any way offensive in China. It is all part of the game of creating ever-widening networks of relationships and favours that the Chinese use to provide security in a notoriously unreliable world.

Compared to the average loner of the western world, the Chinese are very sociable beings. And the focus of all social activities is the common meal. You rarely ever see someone eating alone in a restaurant in China. If you have agreed to meet a Chinese friend for dinner, you can be sure that by the time you arrive half a dozen other friends will be there to give you a big hello. People generally go out to meet, since Chinese flats are often very small, and because an invited guest should be given as lavish a meal as possible. That would just be too much work at home.

Eating together is supposed to create a harmonious atmosphere between diners. Ideally the choice and the order of dishes mirror this harmonious understanding between friends or business partners, and furthermore they mirror the sense of order in the family, the empire and even the whole universe. A central principle of Chinese cuisine is harmony and the balancing of opposites. Chicken, pork, fish, tofu and vegetables are combined to that effect. A yin dish is followed by a yang dish, 'warm' beef is complemented by 'cold' pickled gherkins. Warm and cold here have nothing to do with the temperature at which the dishes are served. They refer to the basic character of certain ingredients in the Chinese culinary universe: peanuts and ginger, for example, are considered 'warm', while tofu and crab are 'cold' even when they reach the table piping hot. This categorisation is a result of the interaction between food and medicine that began over 2,000 years ago in China and shows no sign of weakening. Every spice, every kind of cabbage and every corner of a pig's entrails has its set place in this system. This means that every meal is just what the doctor ordered. Of course it is at the same time deliciously fun. You will find no end of Chinese with a ready supply of wise old sayings. For instance, pickled gherkins remove excess heat, lamb's liver and turtle soup increase masculinity and that 'hot peppers are good for your looks' – as a young Sichuan woman assured me. She was pretty as a picture.

Much has been written about the aesthetic pleasures of a Chinese meal, and about the importance of the colours, smells and flavours of each dish. One characteristic of the ingredients, however, has been criminally neglected by Western observers: the texture – the consistency of the food as it crosses over the threshold and is greeted by the tongue, palate and teeth. European cuisine generally makes use of the sense of touch only in rather crude statements: when we talk about our steak and whether it is tender or tough. What a far more developed range of tactile awareness the Chinese possess! Take that chameleon of Chinese cuisine, tofu – the Chinese people's protein bomb, made from soya beans. Although it tastes of nothing at first, it is highly valued for the different consistencies of its innumerable varieties. One kind of tofu slides softly and smoothly over the back of the tongue, one reveals itself to be porous and juicy, others are stringy like chicken, layered like puff pastry or firm to the bite like a piece of Emmental cheese. Every morsel a new adventure for teeth and tongue. Fish is also often chosen not only for its taste and the fat content of its skin. A Chinese diner will take into consideration whether its meat is firm or soft or whether it melts on the tongue. The firm mandarin fish (*qing zhen gui yu*) for example is excellent in a meal with crispy fried prawn balls and silky tofu topped with a hot Sichuan pepper sauce 'à la pockmarked old woman' (*ma po dou fu*). The Chinese seem to have a particular fondness for gooey, sticky food, especially desserts. Balls formed of sticky rice and filled with a rich sesame or bean paste will have you merrily smacking your lips first, until you suddenly realise your teeth have stuck together. This makes for interesting additions to the conversation round the table.

A word about eating noisily: not only is the

emission of any kind of sound not discouraged, it is actually considered a compliment to the cook and host. It is hard to convince a modern-day visitor to China that this was not always the case. 'Be moderate, do not smack your lips or slurp when eating. No noise should be audible when you eat,' pontificated the Song era philosopher Zhu Xi in his work *What Ignorant Children must Know*. Mao's revolutionaries did away with table manners along with the educated classes, and so children in China today have much more fun, and even adults need not fear a reprimand if they let bones and other inedible bits drop straight from their mouth to the floor, however far the drop.

You can witness this practice in posh restaurants too. Not that every European will approve of it, but it does have something to say for itself on a practical level, since chicken, duck and other poultry is served rather intact. Bones aren't removed. The reader may have heard of those tongue-acrobats who put a simple piece of string in their mouth and after a couple of seconds present a sheepshank knot on their tongue? Apparently from this act one can draw conclusions about the artiste's lovemaking skills. I would suggest, however, that the Chinese tongue-twisters are trained more for deboning poultry than for pleasuring the opposite sex. It is certainly astonishing how masterly the Chinese are at separating meat from bone in their closed mouths. And at what speed! Around the diner's plates and legs there soon rise entire mountain ranges of glistening bits of bone. Once the customers have left, the waitresses move in with shovels and buckets, like a construction crew. Many restaurants have solved the waste removal problem by placing a number of disposable plastic tablecloths on each table. They just need to lift the tablecloth's four corners, tie them together and throw it into the rubbish bin.

It is both inappropriate and pointless to put up any resistance when your host keeps shoving tasty morsels into your mouth, accompanying his endeavours with a cheery '*Chi! Chi! Chi!*' (Eat! Eat! Eat!), as if you were a baby. On the whole though, a foreigner in China is extremely privileged. You are seen as a kind of extraterrestrial, who has no way of knowing the customs of the land. And so you are forgiven everything. Except for one thing: you never empty your bowl in China. That would mean there hadn't been enough food. Hosts would take it as an affront.

One more warning – visitors who arrive in China thinking that the Chinese practically grew up in a rice bowl will be astonished at first, and then perhaps even fall into despair as they try in vain to order a bowl of rice in a restaurant. Most waitresses appear to be deaf to orders of plain rice, and it becomes quite a comedy when helpless foreigners battle to get one. I have fought many such battles myself. In some restaurants where foreigners are regular customers the staff have made allowances by now. This, however, is the exception. The rule is that rice only comes at the end of a good meal, even after the soup. Yet hasn't rice been the staple food for people in this corner of the world – at least in southern China – for 4,000 years? Quite so. But every feast offers the chance to take a break from this everyday staple food. People eating in a restaurant want to enjoy as many good things as possible that they wouldn't normally eat at home. Rice only fills you up, it hampers your appetite.

茶 Cha

Tea

Is drunk almost exclusively in its green, unfermented variety in China. Poets have called it a 'froth of liquid jade'. Neither culturally nor as regards its preparation is tea considered to belong to the same category as coffee. The Chinese fondness for tea can best be compared with the European appreciation of wine. In China tea drinking has been a cultural skill and a passion at least as early as the *Classic of Tea* by the Tang author Lu Yu (728–804). Even the have-nots among my friends find it quite normal to pay the equivalent of £70 for a pound of good tea. Tea leaves are classified by region, soil, plant variety, harvesting time, and by the methods of processing and

112

preparing them. Good restaurants have a tea list, and the tea can be more expensive than the food. Where Westerners often only taste the bitterness caused by the high content of tannic acid, Chinese notice subtle hints of olive (in *longjing* tea), orange (in the *biluochun* variety) and chestnut (in *xinyang maojian*). Like other areas of Chinese life, tea drinking fuses a sophisticated culture with a natural simplicity. Adding sugar, milk or rum to a cup of good tea would evoke a reaction among Chinese tea-lovers similar to ours when we see Chinese yuppies mix red wine and lemonade.

Zen monks have employed tea to approach nirvana. On their way there they made its preparation into a ritual of concentration: 'Three parts against thirst, and seven parts for the senses.' Tea tames unruly temperaments, tea civilises. The water used for green tea shouldn't be boiling hot as it is for black tea. Let it cool to 80 degrees Celsius. Normally the Chinese do not use teabags or filters. They add the loose leaves directly to a big cup or to one of the common screwtop glasses which taxi drivers and shop assistants will never be more than an arm's length away from during their working day. Tea is the fuel that helps most Chinese survive the day. The same tea leaves are infused three or four times before they are thrown away.

The tea plant originally comes from the region today called Yunnan, which means 'South of the clouds'. Traders of the Dutch East India Company brought tea to Europe at the start of the 17th century. The old trading routes have left their traces in the names that different nations gave to the drink. The northern Chinese *cha* has been retained in Portuguese while Russian and Hindi turned it into *chai*. Our tea, the French *thé* and German *Tee* can trace their ancestry back to the Amoy dialect of the southern province of Fujian: there tea is *t'e*.

干杯 *Gan bei!*

Cheers!
Or: Down in one!

One conservative estimate says China currently produces four million tonnes of strong rice and millet spirits. Just a decade ago it was twice as much. That seems to suggest a little-known link between the gradual disappearance of China's socialism and the infirmity of its spirits industry. Yet before anyone tolls its death knell, remember that even today the corridors of officialdom are endless and the civil servants toiling there have enough sense of tradition to keep old customs alive. One of these is the boozing trip to a karaoke salon, paid for by businessmen and others who need to curry official favour. If a single measure of spirit is 25 ml, the equivalent of 160 billion shots are drunk in China every year. Even if we calculate on the basis of the medium-sized water glasses (250 ml) from which people in the interior of China like to drink their rice wine, it would work out to about 16 billion glasses of spirits annually. If we bear in mind the basic rules of Chinese drinking – never drink on your own and never remain silent when you lift your glass – we can conservatively estimate that at least 16 billion times last year the call *gan bei!* rang out across the nation and that each time 'shivers of fear ran down spines and through weaker people's livers' (Hong Kong's *South China Morning Post*). And we haven't even started talking about beer and wine yet.

The phrase *gan bei!* is scarcely conceivable without an exclamation mark. It is a drinking command that asks for the constitution of at least a US marine. Literally it means 'dry your glass', and that is what is expected: not a single drop should be left in it. The more humane custom of *peng* (to drink to someone's health, in more healthy doses) has only survived in refined ladies' mah-jong circles and in the foreigners' reservations. Recently this difference in drinking habits has encouraged the popular belief that China will soon put the West in the shade – an overly rash conclusion that already the Soviet Union once shared.

The weapon of choice in *gan bei!* duels is *bai jiu* (white alcohol), spirits distilled from millet or rice. Maotai and Wuliangye are famous and always welcome. However, they are normally too expensive for the average citizen. There are also many counterfeits of these brands. People in Beijing tell, not without a grudging respect, of the producers who print an 'Anti-Counterfeiting Hotline' number on their bottles – and who, of course, then sit at the other end of the phone to reassure the doubting callers of the authenticity of their product. As a result Beijingers tend to rely on the frightening Erguotou (56 per cent, and only 40 pence for half a litre and four days of amnesia). Erguotou is so cheap that it would not pay to counterfeit it, and it serves the city's inhabitants well in torturing defenceless hostages (such as business partners) and, so I've heard, as motorcycle fuel and cockroach poison. The hip pocket-sized bottle of Erguotou is popular with taxi drivers, policemen and poets. This little green 'one-gulp-pill', as the Chinese call it, costs only three yuan, fits well into the palm of the hand and can in an emergency be used as a Molotov cocktail without the addition of any extra chemicals.

Erguotou is a worthy descendent of the firewater that British sailors came to know in Canton (today's Guangzhou) 170 years ago. It contained alcohol, tobacco juices, sugar and arsenic, as the Reverend Edwin Stevens was shocked to discover. Stevens was the padre at the Seamen's Friend Society mission in Canton. Aboard ship he had the reputation of a puritanical spoilsport. The drink caused 'a degree of inebriety more ferocious than that occasioned by any other spirit,' he thundered. 'It destroys the reason and the senses' and is the cause of 'riotous scenes of the greatest enormity' – qualities that China's distillers can be proud of to this day.

It is the custom of *quan jiu* that often lies at the bottom of such incidents. Its literal meaning is 'to persuade someone to drink'. A good host starts from the tongue-in-cheek assumption that on principle, no one would like to drink and that consequently everyone has to be forced to join in. This leads to a never-ending series of toasts. In China there is no need to wrack your brain for an excuse ('To the Queen!', 'To Mr. Smith!'), you just stand up, hold your own glass up towards the chosen victim and shout 'Come! Come! Come!' or 'Let's dry one!'. In fact, no one ever takes a sip on their own. Every time you raise a glass, you find a partner. Whoever is addressed in this way should take it as an honour, although it certainly bears more the character of an ultimatum than an offer. Objections are out of question, and will be met with an indignant 'Aren't I good enough for you?' or 'Don't you want to give me face?' Escape is no option, unless you're planning on renouncing the friendship or the deal you have just signed.

A popular way of playing your way into intoxication is through games a little like paper-scissors-stone. At a set command the two participants thrust forward a hand, displaying any number of fingers they wish. At the same time they shout a number, trying to guess the total number of fingers displayed by both hands. The loser drinks the next glass. The increasing consumption of alcohol and simultaneous loss of mathematical skill thus mutually benefit each other. A few learned players like to quote their numbers from classic novels like *The Story of the Three Kingdoms*: 'Zhuge Liang's three invitations' they shout with a rush of blood to their faces, or 'The seven arrests of Meng Huo'. Thus they nobly slide into a coma, still the proud ambassadors of a cultured nation.

Beer drinkers also like to challenge each other with *gan bei!*. I once witnessed a famous fashion designer down her freshly poured half-litre glassful in one go without batting an eyelid. The woman came from China's northeastern region, which borders Siberia. Its drinkers are of made of such legendary, sturdy stuff that the Russians themselves never dared to take one step across the border there throughout decades of bitter hostility towards China. In fact beer has now taken its place beside tea as a thirst-quenching drink at mealtimes, its popularity not all dented by the fact that every year several people are injured by exploding bottles. No joke, the problem always tops the list of complaints reported by China's consumers' association. It appears to be a result of cheap producers using old soya sauce and vinegar bottles, which do not always withstand the pressure of the fermenting beer.

But beer has new competition too. Even in Qingdao, where China's most famous beer Tsingtao is brewed, the climate and soil have encouraged the expansion of wine-growing. And so the *yi si ling* (Riesling) and *sha dang ni* (Chardonnay) vines have taken root in China. Actually, grapes have been used to make wine here for 2,000 years, but it took two things to rescue them from a modest life climbing garden walls: the chic Western image of wine and the edict of Premier Li Peng in 1996 that wine too should be served at state banquets. Since then, wine has enjoyed a meteoric rise among the young, upwardly mobile urbanites – the same people who frequent Starbucks cafés and dream of owning a BMW (*bao ma*, precious horse). The Chinese prefer red wine. It is rumoured that Li Peng always mixed some vinegar into his Chardonnay. Vinegar is an all-round miracle drug in China. It fights against both fatigue and high blood pressure, it is said to help the liver to detoxify the body and it cleans out your arteries. When the deadly and previously unknown viral illness SARS broke out in 2003 the price of a bottle of vinegar rocketed to 400 yuan in some regions of southern China. Some young women believe a cocktail of vinegar and red wine helps them lose weight. To many Chinese though, red wine is just too bitter and so they make use of the following recipe: pour in one bottle of Chateau Lafite Rothschild, add the same quantity of Sprite and top it off with a handful of ice cubes and slices of lemon. Now it is ready, as mentioned, to be downed in one. Taming wine with Sprite has a further advantage. Many Chinese cannot hold their alcohol. As is true for dairy products too, a large proportion of the population lacks the enzyme that helps to break it down – in the case of alcohol, the aldehyde dehy- drogenase enzyme. So your drinking partners might go all red after a few sips, or complain of itching all over their bodies, or of headaches. It is characteristic of this brave nation that this natural incompatibility has not led them to abstain from alcohol. Every day countless people fearlessly expose themselves to the possible side effects. One friend wrote this saying down for me: 'Cold spirits are bad for the stomach. Warm spirits damage the liver. But no spirits at all – that would break my heart.' And could he be a noble man who betrays his own heart?

饮食男女 *Yin shi nan nu*

Drink, eat, man and woman
Drawing strength from a shared bowl

Is there anything powerful enough to change China's eating habits? A deadly epidemic perhaps? Questions were raised about chopsticks when the SARS virus hit. As if in a dream, the city was transformed into a strangely peaceful ghost town. To the more curious of us it was as if everything had been frozen and only we could move freely around the scenery. Everyone else had barricaded themselves into their flats with mountains of rice and instant noodles, as if war was imminent. Anyone who had to go out avoided other people. If they met friends they didn't shake hands, but greeted each other as the mandarins once did: their clenched right hand held to their chest, they covered

it with their left hand. Beneath the innocent twit-
tering of the sparrows a muffled carpet of mumbling
spread through the cities that spring. People chatted
through gauze masks tied across their mouths. It was
a time of fear; it was when Hong Ge threw a party in
his flat.

We joked at the time that it must be the only
party being held in the entire city of 14 million
people, and that probably wasn't far from the truth.
It was to be a meal in honour of our friend who was
flying to London the next day to join her husband
– and it was one of those evenings that China lives
for. At six we sat down to eat, at quarter past six we
were toasting each other to congratulate ourselves
on our fearlessness, and by half past seven we were
all drunk. Soon a businessman from Sichuan raised
his glass and accused our friend of deserting China:
'You above all people, as a writer, should stay in your
homeland at this time!' Another friend, a Shanghai
actress, was having none of that. She stood up, also
raising a full glass, and started praising the power
of love that, damn it, even this stupid SARS has to

bow to. *Gan bei!* Down in one! The whole time the hot pot, or 'fire pot' as the Chinese call their fondue, was bubbling away. Its mouthwatering juices, spiced with hot chillies and Sichuan peppers, were constantly being fed with beef, cabbage, bamboo shoots and gold needle mushrooms.

It tasted wonderful. A large spoon leaned against the side of the pot. It was to be used to fish morsels out of the boiling broth. But the guests only made the effort once or twice. They quickly took up their chopsticks again. Soon the chopsticks were happily engaged in swordfights over the vegetable dish and the hot pot, and when the only foreigner at the table shyly asked if there was no risk in us all fishing around in the same pot, the chopsticks only paused a second. What did you say? Surprised faces. Laughter. Then the loud riposte: Never! 'We've eaten like this for thousands of years!' the businessman called from one end of the table. 'And still managed to become the biggest nation on earth.' 'Don't worry,' the shaven-headed musician chimed in, 'This is Sichuan hot pot, it would kill any virus.' A third person added,

'There was a plague in China during the last war, we survived that too.' He lifted his glass for a duel: down in one! And so there everyone was again: busy picking, dunking, fencing, and licking their chopsticks, because you wouldn't want to waste a drop.

I don't want to give the impression that only foreigners were concerned. Zhou Jin for example, a well-known chef specialising in the imperial cuisine, wrote an article about the issue. 'SARS took us by surprise,' Zhou pondered when we met him at the 'Heaven and Earth are One' restaurant. 'But when a catastrophe has hit us, China has always been able to learn lessons from it.' The Beijing chamber of commerce estimated that half of the city's restaurants remained closed for the weeks that the virus held us in its grip. The other half were desolately empty. The waitresses armed with masks and infra-red pistols to check their customers' temperatures didn't help. 'Close your mouths!' a newspaper headline told us. That warning to refrain from spitting was suddenly being taken to mean eating in public places too.

The chairman of the catering trade Han Ming

made two suggestions. So far, she said, Chinese food has been known for its colours, smells and tastes – now it was time to add a further characteristic: cleanliness. No one is likely to oppose that. Cautiously she added a second idea: 'We should also challenge traditional habits such as everyone eating from shared dishes in the middle of the table.' Now that would be a real cultural revolution. Some restaurants did start to serve customers individually after the outbreak of the epidemic. Yet the idea of eating off separate plates is so alien to most Chinese, the concept is so subversive, that the *Beijing Youth Daily* saw it necessary to give its readers careful instructions: 'First the diner uses the shared spoon to put some of the food on the plate in front of him, only then does he use his own chopsticks.' What was that? You should no longer be allowed to reach for food with your own chopsticks and grab the nicest piece of chicken in a fun duel with your neighbour? Nor should you be allowed to then force it on his rice dish or between his lips as a gesture of appreciation?

In this country you can enter a cheap noodle bar

and encounter two complete strangers having a heated 20-minute debate about the correct way to knead, pummel and boil the noodles. Later they will come to an agreement, pleasurably slurping the noodles up from the soup. 'Respect for the noodles' demands this noisy accompaniment, in Liu Qi's opinion. Liu is a columnist for a number of newspapers. He once worked in America as a waiter. It was all a little too elegant and quiet for him there. 'The Americans don't make a sound when they eat,' he reports. 'Now where's the romance in that?' In China intimacy actually thrives on noisy spectacle. Liu had not been out to eat for a whole month when he made an exception for us. 'SARS has already changed the way we eat,' he said over cabbage with assorted wild mushrooms and boiled beef with a pepper dip. 'Many people thank SARS for that.' Suddenly people spent time with their families again, eating together at home every evening. Before the outbreak Liu and his wife had been dining with colleagues or business partners in restaurants every day – not unusual in China. The virus is also said to dissipate quickly in the open air, so the Beijingers discovered picnics. Liu and his wife went to the Fragrant Hills with their friends. 'We rounded off our picnic with a glass of Chinese medicine,' he said. Garlic especially enjoyed new popularity, as it was supposed to kill the virus, especially if munched raw. 'But don't eat more than one whole garlic a day,' advises Liu. He has no sympathy for his countrymen in the South who as a result of the SARS outbreak were forbidden from eating exotic game. The people of Guangzhou are known all over China for eating 'anything with four legs but a chair, anything that flies but a plane, and anything that swims but a submarine.' However, once the first shock had passed, the city's restaurants immediately started advertising the rare black giant salamander on their menus – now claiming that it boosted the immune system and so actually was a remedy against SARS. The salamanders are served raw, as sushi. Chef Zhou Jin is willing to obey the new rules though. He no longer cooks bears' paws, for instance. 'I take camel foot or donkey meat and braise it in apple and cypress juices. It tastes about the same.' Zhou was also one of the first to adopt individual plates. 'Our diners are top politicians and other important people. They are very picky about their hygiene.' Not that it was an easy step for him, as his creations are works of art. 'If you break them up, you destroy them.' Now each dish is first presented to the diners, before the waiters set about destroying it. 'But it will take many years until most people are ready for this,' he believes.

'Like hell they will be!' scoffs a group eating salty baked shrimps in the Hakka Wine House, a restaurant idyllically located on a lake north of Beijing's Forbidden City. 'Great idea,' harrumphs the poet Mang Ke. 'Whoever came up with that must be a total idiot,' the shaven-headed owner Chi Nai adds. He was once a painter. Why does the topic get the friends so excited? Because food in China is never just food: it is the people's soul. 'Do an experiment,' Chi Nai suggests. 'Take our chopsticks away and give us forks instead.' He pokes at the steamed loofah plant. 'You'll be able to watch how we'll just slowly slump listlessly on our chairs. It wouldn't be any fun!' He points at me with his chopstick. 'We do business and hatch plots over meals. If I find you a fish that you've never seen before,' Chi Nai gestures at the perch braised with olives and spring onions, 'then you'll do me the favour that I ask.' But woe betide anyone who wants their own plate! 'Then your neighbour will ask himself: What's he got against me? Does he think I have an infectious disease? And no one wants to be friends with someone odd like that', says Chi Nai. 'How boring!'

And what about the virus? Why wear a face mask, let people spray disinfectant over you, wash your hands thousands of times a day and then have no qualms about poking around with other people in shared dishes? 'Our people have survived any number of epidemics that way,' says Chi Nai. 'If everything is clinically clean, the body can't toughen up. Anyway, we know our friends.' Fittingly foreigners are called *sheng ren*, raw people, while friends and acquaintances are *shou ren*, cooked through. Westerners in general do make a rather raw, even green, impression here. 'Some day all that you will eat from your clean plates will be bean sprouts,' prophesies Chi Nai. 'Then one day you'll fall over, without any strength left.' His popular restaurant was one of the few that did not close for a single day. Moreover, it was full every day. 'My cooks fried until they had tears in their eyes,' he says. 'I'll tell you what helps against SARS – eating, drinking beer and having fun. That's what builds up your immunity!'

The columnist Liu Qi has reconciled himself to the fact that he is part of an incorrigible but pleasure-loving people. 'You Europeans catch your diseases in bed having sex,' he sighs and grins, 'We Chinese catch ours while eating.'

忍 **Ren**

To endure, to withstand

Traditionally the most important of Chinese survival techniques, indispensable under both emperors and communism, in times of famine and political campaigns. It is not by chance that the religion that thrived here took as its principal truth 'life is suffering' (see Gautama Siddhartha, a 6th-century Indian prince who appears in history as the first Buddha – the Enlightened One – revealed to humanity). For thousands of years the common people have applied themselves to no other discipline with as much dedication as to that of eating bitterness. In the process they have trained themselves in patience and a limitless ability to suffer. A product of the fatalism etched in their souls is the oft-heard sigh *mei banfa* ('There's just nothing you can do about it'). It's a sigh used to comment both on the obviously unnecessary chaos at a crossroads that would actually not be very difficult to solve, and on the government's decision to tear down your own house the next morning. People themselves don't have power over their fate. That depends on (a) 'those high up', and (b) time.

What is astonishing though is how fruitfully the Chinese utilize even their fatalism. If the higher powers today demolish a shopkeeper's premises without warning, the shopkeeper won't necessarily drown his sorrows with drink. Instead he will sigh once loudly – and next week open a new shop one corner further down the street. The Chinese live in a different time-universe than Westerners; perhaps that also helps many of them not to fall into depression. Legend has it that Henry Kissinger once asked China's premier Zhou Enlai at the start of the 1970s what he thought of the 1789 French Revolution. 'It is still too early to make a judgment,' the premier is said to have answered. The trick in China is to see the wider sweep of things beyond your own short lifespan. This provides more space for hope. 'That doesn't matter,' a Chinese friend once told me in a heated debate about a terrible injustice. 'If we look back two thousand years and forward a thousand years – it's going to work out ...'

野味 Ye wei

A taste for the wild
The basted donkey

This came in at number three in a sinology website's list of the 'most brutal dishes of China's classical cuisine': take a live donkey, tie it securely next to a pot of bubbling soup. A customer points to the part of the animal that appeals to him or her. The cook then carefully skins the donkey at that part, revealing the flesh beneath. Then he ladles the boiling soup out of the pot and pours it over the meat. Once the meat is cooked well enough for the diner, the chef carves it off the live donkey and serves it. I will spare you the recipes that came in at numbers one and two. I should just mention that the recipes of the basted donkey, the infamous 'brain of a living monkey' (*hou tou*) and the 'three squeaks' (*san zi'r*, a recipe in which living rat embryos play a part) have all been passed down in history and legend. I could however find no evidence of their continued existence in today's China. That is not to say that the technique described above – eating creatures while they're still wriggling about – has completely died out. I still remember vividly the lobster in a hotel restaurant whose powerful claws became part of a children's game. The animal snapped at scraps of paper proffered by little boys, while the parents were already carving their sushi from its abdomen. 'Drunken shrimps' (*zui xia*) are a popular dish. The live shrimps arrive at the table and are placed in an airtight glass bowl with a generous shot of a strong spirit. They then breathe their last in violent spasms. This dish has been immortalised by a Japanese: in his wonderful film *Tampopo* the director Juzo Itami makes the shrimps part of a young couple's foreplay. A young gangster blindfolds his lover and then lets the little creatures jump and twitch around on her naked stomach for several minutes.

Do you want to know how China came across the

St Bernard dog? The St Bernard has not long been known in China, but already some people's enthusiasm for them knows no bounds. It was a certain Professor Du Shaoyue who presented his expert findings of his St Bernard research to the wider public in 1998: 'The perfect meat dog ' he proclaimed on state-run China Central Television. By the following year a *Beijing Youth Daily* headline celebrated 'Good News for the Holiday: a new food for our tables'. The joy was not shared in the St Bernards' homeland. 'Can Switzerland sit back and watch what is being done to St Bernards in China?' exclaimed the Geneva organisation SOS Saint Bernard Dogs with indignation, before giving the expected answer: a clear no. The group threatened a boycott of all Chinese restaurants.

Not far from our flat, East Beijing's Gourou Wang does not need to worry about customers yet. The restaurant's name means 'The King of Dog Meat'. Tender dog breast in an oyster sauce and red-cooked dog's knuckle can be savoured there. The most popular winter dish is the dog fondue. 'It's very warming,' says the waitress. The customers are Chinese and

Koreans – both cultures have had dog on the menu as far back as can be remembered. Chronicles reveal that over 2,000 years ago the Han emperors liked to serve a stew of dog meat and sow-thistles between a dish of panther breast and a bowl of roasted owl. Soon medical manuals were spreading the theory that dog meat was good for the liver. Even today in the system of culinary-medical classification dog is considered to be a 'yin' meat with the particular characteristic of warming the body (which is why the Chinese eat dog mainly in the winter). At the same time dog meat absorbs dangerous 'fire' (which is why the Koreans like to tuck in mainly in summer). You should, however, never use spirits in a dog recipe, a Ming era book warns, otherwise you risk haemorrhoids.

Yet, unlike cattle and pigs, dogs were never bred on a large scale – until the St Bernards arrived. 'There are many kinds of dog in the world, but so far there is no meat dog,' says Professor Du Shaoyue in the educational film, before stating triumphantly, 'No dog would be a better sire for such a race than the St Bernard.' Romantic piano music starts playing, the camera pans slowly across a group of pups clumsily stumbling around in the grass, and we hear the advantages of the race being praised: its size, its gentle nature, the size of the litter, their robustness, their quick rate of growth. It is generally the offspring of the St Bernards and Chinese bitches that is eaten – the purebred St Bernard sires are too expensive. *The Animal and Fish Breeding Newspaper* complains about 'import difficulties', as 'foreigners have certain reservations about the custom of eating dog meat in some regions of our country'.

These reservations are shared, by the way, by not a few Chinese too. The gourmet and author Li Yu had already by the 17th century campaigned for beef and dog meat to be taken off the menu. Cows and dogs are friends of man, he said. A survey in Beijing and Shanghai revealed that while 43 per cent of those surveyed had eaten dog meat at least once, the majority would never consider it. The teacher Guo Lizhen is one of those. She owns a white Pekinese called A Pang (Chubby). Almost 200,000 Beijingers have a dog now – as a pet, not as emergency rations for cold winter's days. 'He is so clever, and he understands me,' Guo says. Guo has been served dog fondue only once. Her boyfriend at the time devoured it. She got angry with him. 'It's cruel.' She remembers with a shudder how he ate everything in the pot. He was French. Traditionally dog meat has been eaten in the regions near the border with Korea and, of course, in the southern Chinese province of Guangdong. 'Honestly, I couldn't say what the difference between eating a calf and a St Bernard is,' admitted a Swiss diplomat in Beijing to me in private. 'Switzerland has to think carefully whether it really wants to take on the role of an international St Bernard protector, just because the dogs are genetically from there.' It has yet to take that the step.

One of the major fears of Western visitors to China seems to be that a morsel of dog or snake could furtively or accidentally be slipped into their lunch. Let me reassure you that in all my years in China that has not happened to me once, for a very simple reason: all the things that seem particularly revolting to you are in fact delicacies to the Chinese, and so they are much more expensive than pork, beef or chicken. If you hanker for an owl breast, a marmot tail or a bit of camel's hump, you will have to ask for it. That does not mean that your Chinese hosts won't rustle up all kinds of surprises for you – maybe because you are the guest of honour, or maybe because the host simply enjoys watching your face as a twisting silkworm is pushed between your lips on your neighbour's chopsticks. But silkworms, and similar dainties like scorpions, grasshoppers etc, are as a rule recognised to be exotica and so can be politely refused. A simple *bu xi guan* ('I'm not used to that') on your part should do the job. More stubborn hosts you can fend off with a brave volley of *gan bei!*.

When judging Chinese eating habits, Westerners should remember two things. Firstly, a large proportion of the dishes that we eye with suspicion had their origins in the continual struggle against hunger that this people had to fight for millennia, forcing it to take advantage of every source of calories. This is why they chew chicken or duck's feet, why they serve cow's tendons, pig's ears and brains. (Not that similar discoveries can't be made in Europe. In some old Bavarian inns in my home region roasted cow's udder is served. I still haven't plucked up the courage to try it.) Secondly, there are immense cultural divides inside China itself. We Europeans generally find ourselves in the same camp as the northern Chinese. They shake their heads at the eating habits of their southern brethren just as much as we do. You will see foyers crammed full of cages and aquariums that give the impression of an exhibition of *National Geographic*'s collected articles of the last five decades. But these exhibits are found almost exclusively in restaurants serving the cuisine of Guangzhou. My Beijing friends would never touch the dishes offered in these restaurants, be it 'Red-cooked pangolin' (a scaly ant-eater) or 'Rat roasted in sugarcane with black beans'. Not that they could afford most of them anyway. The English-language *China Daily* recently published a big photo of three-year-old Zhou Ran adding her name to a petition: 'Zhou Ran promised to protect wild animals and not to eat them', the caption said.

Until the Zhou Rans of the country have grown

up though, and become its opinion leaders, trips to China can in good conscience only be recommended to members of that species that currently occupies the top of the food chain.

四害 *Si hai*

The Four Evils
Rats, sparrows, mosquitoes and flies

Beijing television has a programme called 'Documentaries'. 'Today we'd like to talk about the protection of animals,' a presenter said recently. The story was about a injured golden eagle that had been found by a farmer on the southern outskirts of Beijing. A little fairy tale unfolded. She took the bird to three old vets who in the following months tried everything to restore the bird to health. For half a year a camera team followed the vets' moving efforts. One of them went to the market every day to buy the raptor live mice. A salesgirl would fish them from the bottom of a container and offer a squeaking handful to the vet. At supper time the second vet would hold a twitching, panic-stricken dove in front of the eagle, who apparently was still suffering from a delicate appetite. The third gently massaged its broken wing. Finally the much-anticipated day had arrived: the eagle had regained its health and was to be released as the cameras rolled and the excited public clapped. But television viewers waited in vain for pictures of the flight to freedom. Instead, the programme cut to the slightly embarrassed presenter in the studio, who announced that a 'terrible thing' had occurred. No one had considered that on these same days the Fengtai district had its annual crusade to wipe out rats, and – how should he put it? – it had not been to the eagle's advantage that he had finally regained his appetite. The eagle plunged from the sky, sank his claws into one of the dead rats that seemed to have been laid out for his consumption. He devoured it and the rat poison inside it, and died almost instantly. The dispatch closed with pictures of the crying farmer and the dumbstruck rescuers. Then the studio camera panned solemnly and there he stood: the proud eagle with his penetrating stare, his wings spread wide, full of sawdust. Stuffed. Few environmental fairy tales in China can claim a happy ending.

So the story turns out to be more of an allegory, not least because a report that was announced as being a piece of environmental education completely failed to draw the obvious conclusion: that the chances of survival of such magnificent birds might have something to do with an attitude that endorses yearly state-organised campaigns to poison, drown or otherwise kill organisms considered inferior. I admit, to my shame, that I have taken part in such slaughters myself, namely cockroach hunts. The little animals can, however, in China's warmer and more humid regions, grow to such a size that they would even make entomologists keep their distance. As flatmates they can become rather unpleasant. When, for example, having sailed in through an open window, they wait in ambush inside the toe of the shoe that you will slip your bare foot into the next morning. Or when they pinch your shoulder so hard in the night that you wake up with a start and throw your bedclothes across the room in fright. Both have happened to me.

They are not only big, they are also remarkably tough. The strongest blacksmith can smash his hammer down on one, there might be a cracking and splattering, but if you leave the room just for a moment to fetch a broom, you'll drop it in surprise when you get back – no sign of the murder victim. No more than a flattened mix of scales and goo that will still have managed to drag itself off to shelter. This hint of immortality gives an almost mythical dimension to the struggle between *homo sapiens* and the cockroach. It is not by chance that the weaponry supplied by China's chemical industries bears poetic names. The 'Last Supper' is one of the more famous agents, but not the most effective. Years of experiments conducted in my circle of acquaintances allow me to report with some authority that although the common cockroach may well survive nuclear warfare, it definitely will not survive the powder sold in Beijing under the proud name of 'King of Genocide'.

The yearly crusade against cockroaches is organised at the highest level by special 'patriotic committees for the propaganda of hygiene'. It hits billboards and the front pages of newspapers, and becomes the lead item on local television news. We know that time of year has come round again when the management service of our apartment building posts one of those notices that I so like to collect and frame: 'Honoured Residents! The icy winter is over again. Warmth floods around us and sunshine cradles inside us. Spring is marching on, the trees are in bud, the flowers in bloom and the cockroaches are experiencing a boom … ' Generally such a notice will end with the appeal for every family to make its way to the ammunition depot as soon as possible to collect their allotted ration of cockroach or rat poison. Anyone who does not turn up will receive a phone call, politely reminding them of their patriotic duty to join the hunt. I never quite figured out why such a hygiene-related action is considered patriotic in the first place. Certainly Mao Zedong made it clear to them long ago that they aren't legitimate inhabitants of the People's Republic of China.

Long before Mao there were Taoists in China. They believed that an ideal life was led by a person at one with nature. Then there were the Buddhists, who did not want to harm a single hair on the head of any living being. And finally you had the Confucians, who generally held power. They did not see any harm in using nature and controlling it, but they were concerned above all with doing everything in moderation. Mao Zedong – revolutionary, utopian and tyrant – broke with all of them. The poet Mao saw 'an inexhaustible source of joy' in 'struggling with earth and man'. He wanted to mould both according to his will. He had a socialist paradise in mind, in which there was no place for the old laws of his country – or those of physics for that matter. Mao played God and started a war: against both the human soul and nature. 'If we order the mountain to lower its head, it must do so,' Mao Zedong wrote in 1958. And so he ordered the 'conquest of nature'. Mao started a massive extermination campaign. He exhorted his people to 'wipe out the four evils'. For Mao these were rats, sparrows, mosquitoes and flies. And while things were terrible enough for the rats, they could be glad they did not have wings, because what the Chinese did to the sparrows that year was even worse. It was a crazy example of what Mao meant when he encouraged his people to imitate the 'foolish old man' who in an old legend moves a whole mountain with his bare hands and shows nature what's what. Mao's sparrow hunt also reveals the power of his words, how deeply China was in the thrall of its Great Chairman and in the clutches of his organisation. The party said 'Kill!' so everybody went out onto the streets and fields, carrying all the pots, gongs and drums they could muster. At a set command they all began to shout and make a frightening racket. They kept this up for days, until the frightened and exhausted sparrows, that did not dare land anywhere actually fell from the sky, dead. The effect was soon felt: not long after the country was infested with insects. Mao and his men were not concerned. 'Bring cereals from the mountain peaks,' the propaganda trumpeted, 'bring cereals from the seas.' There was no need to worry about nature: 'As people obey Chairman Mao, so nature will obey people.' The earth wasn't about to do so though, and let between 30 and 50 million people starve to death.

When Mao died in 1976 he left a broken people and a violated land. There were barren hillsides where forests had stood, deserts where prairies had been, there was eroded soil, broken dams and imploding ecosystems. The party had proudly celebrated Mao's thought as a 'spiritual atomic bomb'. What a shame for China that it was exploded over their own country. China is still struggling with the legacy of devastation it wrought, not only on the country's land but also on its spirit and soul.

Naturally, even in China there have been environmentalists for a long time, protesting against the poaching of Tibetan antelope as well as against the slaughter of the St Bernard. A Chinese activist in Beijing once explained to me the seeming indifference to animals in her country: 'Where people have been treated as cruelly as they have in our country, how can we expect people to feel sympathy for animals?' There is no animal protection law in China – yet, added the activist. She says her organisation has noticed an increasingly positive response from the authorities.

红塔山 *Hong ta shan*

The Mountain of the Red Pagoda

A cigarette brand from the southwest province of Yunnan. For seven years in a row it was China's most valuable brand name, only losing the top spot in 2003 to the globally-expanding household appliance producer Haier. No wonder it is so valuable: China is the world's largest market for tobacco. Around 350 million people smoke here – 95 per cent of them men. Until now they have smoked almost exclusively local brands, including the famous *Zhonghua* (China) and *Xiao Xiongmao* (Little Panda). The latter was the vice of the now dead patriarch Deng Xiaoping, who came from Sichuan, the home of the panda. Deng allowed himself two packs a day and lived to

92, a fact that contributed to the supposition among Chinese – widely held until quite recently – that smoking was good for your health. (For many years China's top football league was officially called the 'Marlboro League', after its sponsors.) Smoking is also a social act in China, a cigarette is often offered before a handshake. Nowadays the government warns people about the dangers of smoking. Not an easy thing to do for them, given that the tobacco industry is the country's largest taxpayer and employs millions of people.

The exclusive Little Pandas were reserved for the members of the ruling circle for decades. Only after Deng's death were they made available to the wider population. A pack costs between 25 and 35 yuan. There are other brands that cost less than one yuan. They all have beautiful names. One traditional brand is called Red Double Happiness. Two of the newer ones are called Shangri-La and Viagra (in Chinese: *Wei ge*, literally: 'powerful brother').

过节 *Guo jie*

Celebrations
Eating the moon

The Chinese do not only eat swallows' nests and shark's fin, they also eat the moon. They have a much closer relationship to it than we sun worshippers. Since the fall of the last emperor in 1911, China has officially followed the solar year in its calendar as we do. Yet the old lunar calendar, also called the farmer's almanac, still plays an important role. Not only are the major festivals such as New Year and Mid-Autumn celebrated according to the lunar calendar, many traditional-minded Chinese schedule important events on auspicious days of the lunar year. They will not cut their hair, take out a loan or get married without first consulting the calendar. The Chinese state officially scorns such practices as dangerous superstition. But in Taiwan you will find daily columns in the newspapers, telling readers that 'today the moon is ideal for recovering debts and building a house', but unfavourable for 'installing ovens'. (At breakfast in Taipei I once opened the newspaper to read that 'Today is a good day for: nothing'.) In recent years these old customs that stem from farmers' observations of the moon are experiencing something of a renaissance in Europe too. Some people now cut their fingernails in one phase of the moon, and their chives in another. But it is in no way such a natural part of everyday life as it is in China.

For over a thousand years the Chinese have baked a little cake that is as shiny and round as the moon in its finest night of the year – the night that closes the fifteenth day of the eighth month of the traditional lunar calendar. It arrives well into autumn, when nature is dying – reason enough for the Chinese of yore to also carry out their executions at this time of year. Not that they forgot to party. China's Moon Festival takes place on the evening of that day when the moon is farthest from the earth. When the sky is clear, people congregate in parks and on terraces. Children carry lanterns, adults hunt for moonlit verse, and everyone looks out for the many creatures with which Chinese mythology has colonized the moon. There is the toad, there is a hare, and naturally there is China's lady in the moon, Chang E, who drank her husband's elixir of immortality and then floated out of the window and up to the moon. Chang E has given her name to China's programme of lunar exploration, which is intended to bring China new fame as a space-faring nation.

The Chinese sing of the moon in the heavens and eat its image here on earth. There are reports that by the time of the Tang dynasty (618–907) the noble-women sweetened their full moon strolls with the little cakes. Every bite in one of these cakes no bigger than the palm of a child's hand is a surprise. Normally you will bite into a traditional filling of sugar and lotus seeds, or sugar and bean paste. Nowadays pretty much anything could be inside: nuts, dates, vanilla ice cream from Häagen-Dazs, coffee, ham or bacon. Moon cakes are the Chinese equivalent to Kinder Eggs: You never know what is inside. Cinnamon flower paste perhaps? Oh no, pork and duck's egg this time.

In the weeks leading up to the festival you can barely move in shops and department stores for all the cartons of moon cakes stacked everywhere. Yet mysteriously, it is hard to find anyone who actually likes to eat them. Chinese friends will react at any mention of the things with a 'terrible stuff!', or 'sickeningly sweet!', followed by a tragic sigh. The average moon cake will block your digestive system and extinguish your appetite for days afterwards. They have the density of a black hole. And if they had a hole in the middle you could just as well use them as dumb-bells.

As if that were not reason enough to avoid moon cakes, recently the land was rocked by a moon cake scandal. The Guang Sheng Yuan bakery in Nanjing, famous for its cakes for over 80 years, was caught being a little too frugal even by Chinese standards. Authorities discovered the company was using last year's leftover filling for the new cakes. Moon cake sales all over China collapsed. It was a catastrophe for an industry with a yearly turnover of some 20 billion yuan. (Today it is eight to nine billion yuan, says the Chinese bakers' association.) To me though it seemed as though half the country had only been waiting for an excuse – which the scandal thankfully gave them – to finally rid themselves of moon cakes. 'Moon cakes are a victim of China's modernisation,' one of our friends said. 'Lots of things that we liked when we were children we now can't stand.' The Beijing TV producer Ying Da has a particular motive for avoiding them – a childhood trauma. 'I've hated moon cakes as far back as I can remember,' says Ying Da, normally an amicable character. He gave China its first sitcoms. His aversion stems from the fact that the cakes are also a symbol of xenophobia – or of patriotic appeal to the people, it all depends which side you are on. It derives from a 14th century legend when China suffered under the less than gentle rule of the Mongols. Chinese rebels are said to have conspired to revolt in an unusual way. They baked a note inside the cakes, its secret message still known

160

to children today: 'On the 15th of the month kill the Tartars!' The Tartars being the Mongols. The same battle cry was later directed towards the Manchus, who were also horse-riding nomads from the north. They gave China the Qing dynasty (1644–1911). Today, less than a century after their fall, the Manchus and the Han Chinese cannot for the most part be distinguished any more as separate peoples, but Ying Da was always aware that he was a descendant from a Manchu family. 'Every Moon Festival the other children had fun shouting "Kill the Tartars!" I for one won't be shedding any tears for the moon cakes.'

The moon cakes' modern role is to be given away, and not only to your friends. You can find anything in the prettily wrapped boxes, from expensive tea leaves to gold coins. Even wristwatches and mobile phones have been known to tumble out. It is a discreet way of showing your appreciation to an acquaintance in local government or to your boss. Offices and government departments buy hundreds of boxes of moon cakes each year. The Shanghai producer Yuanchu is not worried about market developments. 'No one has to eat moon cakes any more,' marketing manager Qiao Keqin says happily, 'but everyone has to give them as presents now.'

The Spring Festival is even more important than the Moon Festival. China's New Year's Eve is the one day of the year on which the whole family meets at home for a feast. It is the evening before the lunar calendar launches into a new year. After the empire's fall the Gregorian calendar was adopted in 1912 and subsequently what was once known as the New Year Festival was renamed the Spring Festival. To get an idea of its importance and the pandemonium that it creates in families, imagine Christmas and Easter falling on the same day. One of the simplest and cheapest dishes possible, *jiao zi*, has pride of place in the New Year's Eve feasting. It is Italian ravioli's distant ancestor.

The fun thing about Spring Festival *jiao zi* is that the cook is not left alone in the kitchen. Everybody helps. The family members normally meet in the late afternoon at the house of the parents or the eldest brother. The presents of fruit, cigarettes and expensive

Maotai rice spirits are placed in a corner, everyone grabs a stool and helps with *bao jiao zi*, making *jiao zi*, Chinese dumplings. Basically you need to squeeze a dough disc as skilfully as you can around a spoonful of filling. The latest jokes about the president are told and everyone tries to outperform the others. Ideally the *jiao zi* will look like a sickle moon. Real pros lay the ingredients on their hand and then snap the hand into a fist. A foreigner, mustering all his or her concentration, rarely manages to make more than an amoeba-like dough monster. Although these are greeted with encouraging words, the foreigner soon takes the president's place as the butt of everyone's jokes and finds that no one else will eat the sorry creations. *Jiao zi* are made with a variety of fillings. There is the minced beef and onion combination, there are minced pork and fennel, chives and egg, spinach, mushroom or shrimp. At the Spring Festival families prefer the traditional filling: minced pork and cabbage, seasoned with ginger, spring onions, salt and pepper.

There are in fact two meals: a banquet of a dozen courses starts the evening off with meats, fish and vegetables. Then on the dot of midnight, after the first rounds of mah-jong and after everyone has laughed and made nasty remarks about the New Year's Eve gala, the TV event of the year, the dumplings are thrown into boiling water. This is the moment when the old and new years meet, when the rooster makes way for the dog, and a year later the dog for the boar. People eat a few cold appetizers to start with – roasted peanuts, cold meats, marinated pig's ear and sliced pickled jellyfish. Then everyone descends on the steaming *jiao zi*. You eat them with a dipping sauce suited to your own taste, mixing vinegar, soya sauce, garlic, chilli and sesame oil. After midnight the lucky inhabitants of the suburbs can go out and celebrate with rockets and bangers. The Beijing government has for years strictly forbidden any fireworks inside the Fourth Ring Road – and that in the capital of the nation which invented them! For a long time I thought it was just one of the Beijing bureaucrats' typical spoilsport rules. Then a friend invited me to spend New Year's Eve at her house. She lived near to the airport, and what we experienced after eating *jiao zi* had more in common with a manoeuvre of the People's Liberation Army gone awry than with any New Year's celebrations I knew. There was one difference though: these people were more heavily armed than normal soldiers, and they were blind drunk. Not only that, instead of having two opposing sides, it was everybody against everybody. I did not see much of the slaughter. When one rocket came screaming horizontally into the cardboard box that we were using to store our arsenal, I crept behind a jeep at the edge of the battlefield. That was where I was an hour later, when my friends – happily laughing, and red-cheeked after their winter sport – found me: crouched down with my hands over my ears and my eyes screwed shut. As if I was one of the spirits that were meant to be banished.

京骂 *Jing ma*

The Beijing curse

No, this does not refer to an old curse rising from the depths of the imperial vaults. The Beijingers are infamously foul-mouthed, much to the local government's embarrassment. The most popular example is the exclamation '*Sha bi!*', which combines a denigration of the addressee's intelligence with a vulgar reference to a woman's private parts. *Sha bi!* is closely related to the roar of approval *Niu bi!* (roughly equivalent to: great, super, wicked), which settles for the private parts of the cow. *Sha bi!* and *Niu bi!* reveal their full power when the echo of tens of thousands of football fans reverberates through the stadiums. It is mortifying to the city's Department for Spiritual

Civilisation, particularly when they look forward to the 2008 Olympics. So they make valiant but vain efforts to re-educate residents. 'Say no to the Beijing curse!' lights up the video screen of the Workers' Stadium before every football match now. *'Sha bi!'* comes the reply from the terraces. 'Follow the game in a civilised way!' is the next slogan. *'SHA BI! SHA BI!'* scream 30,000 enthusiastic voices. The department would like to persuade fans to sing 'happy songs' instead. The fans don't give a damn what the department would like. Beijing curses caused some embarrassment during the 2002 World Cup when they appeared in *Fifa Football 2002*, the official World Cup football computer game. The game's American production company simply pointed out that the sounds for each nation had been recorded live on location.

素质 *Su zhi*

Quality and class
Improving the citizenry

The Chinese word for 'state' is *guojia*, which literally means 'state family'. The state, like the family, is ruled by patriarchs at the top (be it an emperor or a politburo) who look after their children, the people. As incredible as it may sound, one reason why communism was able to take root in China was exactly because it seemed to echo an ancient Chinese idea of utopia.

According to Chinese tradition the ruler has two principal tasks. One is to care for the people's material needs. The Communists may have been the first government in Chinese history who actually fulfilled the old philosophers' theoretical requirement of an ideal leader. Every Chinese was given his 'iron rice bowl'. For a few years at least, China had never seemed nearer to its old dreams of 'great peace' (*tai ping*) and 'great equality' (*da tong*). This is why many common Chinese people look back on the years under Mao with a great deal of nostalgia. 'In Mao Zedong's time we lived in tiny flats. We don't any more – but things were still much better then,' an official from Ningxia province recently told me. 'Because we all had the same-sized flats. It's true, I have a big flat now. But some of my colleagues have much bigger flats than me. How can that be fair?' The friendly official in his mid-fifties is originally from Beijing. He only ended up in the wretchedly poor desert province of Ningxia because he had been sent there as a young man, by Mao's Red Guards. Yet the equality in poverty of those years in his eyes seems to have been more than fair trade for the brutality and madness of Mao's policies.

China's government still plays this old song, when it replies to its Western critics on human rights issues: the government must first ensure that all Chinese are 'warm and full'. Calls for the 'Solution to the Warm-

and-Full-Issue' (*wen bao wen ti*) are a common rallying-cry at Communist Party congresses.

When the subjects are finally full, China's rulers and the cooperating elite will then answer the call to educate them. The emperors of old exhorted their people through countless edicts to practise filial piety and chastity. They created monuments to women who, when their cities fell, had preferred to take their own lives rather than fall into the hands of their enemies. These 'chastity gates' can still be seen today all over the country. The new Communists have it made their goal to put an end to swearing, to pushing to the front of queues and to shopping in pyjamas. To this end there are Committees for Patriotic Hygiene Campaigns and Departments for Spiritual Civilisation all over the country. In Beijing there even resides an Authority for the Promotion of Morality. Every other day in the Party's *People's Daily* newspaper you will find headlines such as 'Raise the quality (*su zhi*) of our citizens!' The prophets of doom return again and again to the lack of *su zhi*, which describes a mixture of good character, education, tactfulness and virtuousness – in fact everything a person supposedly needs to become a finer citizen.

Two groups are most active in admonishing the subjects to be better Chinese: (a) the party cadres who unfortunately often themselves display such low morals; and (b) the intellectuals, usually from better backgrounds, who at the same time are masters of the *pai ma pi* technique, the obsequious 'stroking the horse's arse'. This leads us back to (a), because in China as in the West the arses getting stroked are the fattest ones, the ones belonging to the powerful people. But even China's scattered democrats often blame the slow progress of their mission on the lack of *su zhi* of their compatriots. The complaints are commonly directed at China's rural folk, which still account for more than two-thirds of the population. To my knowledge, China's government has yet to expose itself to an independent assessment of its own quality. The ones accusing people of lacking enough class like to point to the state of public toilets. This is a social flaw that the government recently took action to change by hosting the Fourth World Toilet

Summit in Beijing. There the chairperson of the Taiwan Toilets Association could be heard lecturing on 'The Humane Toilet', and the Malaysian delegate on 'Differing Toilets for Different Cultures'. Another area of shame for the state is the stubborn absence of a Chinese Nobel Prize winner (while the winner of the 2000 Nobel Prize for Literature, Gao Xingjian, who lives in exile in Paris is stubbornly ignored by Beijing).

And then there is the uninhibited habit of spitting. It can catch you unawares wherever you are. You might be on a sleeper train to Suzhou when suddenly you are awakened in the wee hours of the morning by a choir of refreshed little dragons, energetically clearing their fiery throats over the sinks and the spittoons. If you are privileged enough to witness the real pros in action, you will first recognise them by the gentle hum rising ominously from the back of their throats. That is the signal that they are ready to launch – it also is your final warning and last chance to take cover. Soon the humming will swell to a gurgling and finally a roaring not unlike the sound of an aeroplane taking off. Every muscle from the stomach to the palate is pressed into service as the exercise reaches a hissing crescendo. Then, within the blink of an eye, the hissing stops, before the flight path is cleared in a final cathartic eruption. Normally you will already have fled the scene by then, or at least buried your head under the table, so that it is just a distant echo you hear of the smack of phlegm when it hits the ground.

The custom is an old one, and as deeply rooted, as China's newspapers often complain. Even in 1793 Lord MacCartney, His Majesty's ambassador to China, noticed on a visit to Peking that the imperial mandarins spat in every chamber they encountered. Today the mandarins are ashamed of the habit and want the general populace to abstain too – and not for the first time. Every few years the hygiene men clean their weapons in preparation for another salvo. 'One idea must be lodged in every mind,' wrote an official from Guangzhou during the last campaign: 'Spitting is illegal!' Cities everywhere have raised the fines for spitting: you now pay 50 yuan in Guangzhou and

Beijing, if you are caught. If, that is! It is not easily done. Collecting evidence (the rules in Guangzhou demand a photo of the scene of the crime) is as much of a headache as the fining itself. 'Some people run away, others shout "I've got money, so fine me!" and throw the money on the ground, ' says an official named Huang. Most people just cannot see what is so bad about the custom. Take the old man in Beijing's Sun Altar Park who, as we watch, waters the weeds with a high fluid arc. 'It was itching in my throat. So what?' he says with a shrug of his shoulders.

A Beijing newspaper advertises an Anti-Spitting Hotline. When you call 68516110 a Ms Ye from the city's Eastern Surveillance Team answers the phone. What would you do if I reported a culprit? 'We'd send a team straightaway. They'd be there in half an hour.' Wouldn't he be long gone by then? 'Then we might put up a sign: No Spitting!' China is covered with these signs, some of them went rusty decades ago. The war on spitting is as old as the republic. Sun Yat-sen, the revolutionary who brought down the last emperor, was just as vociferously opposed to wild spitting (*luan tu*) as was later the government under Deng Xiaoping, the architect of China's reforms and opening. It didn't exactly help that Deng even showed his love of spitting in front of state visitors and TV cameras. At least his well-aimed spit always landed in his spittoon. Deng held a belief that was long popular in Europe too, and still holds widespread acceptance in China today: one should regularly release the body's bottled up gases and juices. So spitting, like burping and passing gas, is considered good for your health.

To be fair, things are changing. There are more and more converts, like the friend of mine whose girlfriend made him stop spitting 10 years ago. 'It's quite an unforgettable experience,' he reminisces, 'when you are sitting on a train and find that what has just left the throat of the man two rows ahead of you is now flying back through your open window.' My friend today runs one of Beijing's finest restaurants. Today the government does not only fine people, it also appeals to their sense of hygiene. The *Evening Daily* prints anti-spitting ditties ('Spitting is so bad to do/ Nasty germs lay in wait for you') and distributes free little plastic bags – mobile spittoons, as it were. The People's Republic's press has always followed the line its government has whispered to it. Today the press still sees the readers' moral education as one of its major duties. The *Beijing Youth Daily*, the city's best and most widely-read newspaper, publishes a daily cartoon under the heading 'A little extra we need to be civilised'. This time the gentle reminder features the picture of a young man boarding a public bus, effectively elbowing both of the elderly women on each side of him. That is certainly not civilised, and is accordingly criticized in the accompanying commentary.

Are any of these efforts successful? In the heyday of the anti-spitting campaign we witnessed in one day: a chic young sales assistant spitting out of the door of her boutique, an officer spitting in front of his marching soldiers, a cyclist who spat right in front of us. You find it disgusting? You are not, I hope, one of those people who always carry around a little square of paper or cloth, into which you then blow your nose – even at the dining table? Before wrapping up the contents and putting it back into your pocket, where you'll carry it around all day long? To the Chinese that is disgusting. 'And let's be honest,' the converted restaurant owner said, 'You Europeans spit too. I see it at every football match: in slow motion and close-up.'

Spitting and swearing are number one and two on an official list of bad habits in the city that Beijing's government wants to eliminate. When the mayor presented the list to the public he said it represented 'a great weakness in our civilisation'. The mayor made a solemn oath that by 2008 when the Olympic Games come to Beijing the city would be worthy of them. We should mention that Beijing's old rival Shanghai has published such a list for 10 years now, although the Shanghai one only comprises seven bad habits, in comparison to Beijing's 12. You could consider that a clue to which city thinks it is further along the path towards moral respectability.

Both cities also target other customs not on the lists. Beijing beat the drum one summer against the *bang ye*, the 'shirtless men'. Principally fathers and grandfathers, on hot summer days you see them sitting in front of their dwellings in the old town with their trouser legs rolled up and their chests bare. Without any air-conditioning it is almost unbearable inside their sweltering houses. They will with one hand proudly slap their stomach, as if to reassure themselves that it is still there, and with the other waggle a bamboo fan to cool it down. Their own grandfathers no doubt spent their hot summer days the same way under the Mongol rulers, and their grandchildren in turn would have enjoyed the same privilege if it weren't for the *Beijing Youth Daily* which, along with the authorities, one summer decided to deny visitors to the city the sight of naked bellies. Hordes of volunteers and reporters descended on the astounded men, educating them on the spot about the uncivilised nature of their activity and forcing T-shirts on them which concealed their proud masculine beauty. The slogan on the T-shirts read 'A civilised Beijing starts with me'. Riding my bike through the *hutongs*, the narrow old alleyways, I could scarcely take my camera out of my bag in those weeks without having three *bang ye*s dive behind piles of coal. 'No photos! Or else we'll end up in the paper and be blamed for giving Beijing a bad image!' one called out, panic showing in his eyes.

While Beijing tries to throw shirts over its men, the Shanghai government is trying to rip an item of clothing from its citizens: pyjamas. It is not that the local government has something against pyjamas *per se*, they just don't want them out on the streets. After all, Shanghai tries so hard to be a cosmopolitan city. Formula 1 has already come to the city. In 2010 it expects millions of visitors for the World Expo. Amazing buildings of glass and steel are shooting towards the heavens – but down below people are still walking around in their pyjamas in broad daylight. They wander to the market in their pyjamas and they buy dim sum at a food stall in them. You will see the classic prison stripes, frilly pyjamas, plaid fleece and pyjamas embroidered with teddy bears. This tradition is no doubt related to the sultry Shanghai summers. It meant that people often had no choice but to make their beds outside on the pavements. There they soon made friends with their neighbours' nightwear. Pyjamas had thus conquered a new space, and over time they became to Shanghai's old town what sweat pants are to the more proletarian parts of European cities. Today there are little pyjama shops all over Shanghai. They even bring out new winter collections every year – warmly-lined pyjamas with the patterns of the season. The Shanghainese do have a reputation to live up to. 'People here don't just throw on any old pyjamas when they go out,' noticed the fashion editor Li Yan. 'They wear their most stylish set.'

Apart from issues of clothing, the government has one great desire for its citizens: 'Be a friendly Shanghainese!' This is the title of a campaign that aims to do the impossible by the time of the Expo 2010. When an American survey recently placed Shanghai as the eighth friendliest of 23 major cities worldwide, the *Shanghai Star* neatly summarised people's reactions in the city: 'Only a foreigner could have made this list.' Reading this my first assumption was to think that the Shanghainese felt they had been hard done by, and deserved a better ranking. Not at all. The article went on to explain in detail why the Shanghainese are considered arrogant, selfish and cold by their fellow Chinese – and why this was absolutely true, why in fact eighth place was much too flattering a rating. The reporters backed up their claims with an experiment. They dropped a stamped addressed envelope, as if by accident, to see how long it would take before a helpful person popped it in a post box. 'Twenty minutes later our reporters returned. To their surprise they discovered that the envelope had been opened, and the 60 fen stamp stolen,' the newspaper reported. Admittedly, this was not a particularly representative investigation, but to the journalists it obviously seemed typical of their city.

On the one hand, one can be grateful that the government's moralising is just a faint echo of Mao's plans for a 'new man' which turned the whole country into one giant re-education camp. On the other hand, you would be forgiven for crying 'Hypocrite!' when faced with the Communist Party's moral pose. This again leaves you with at least two possible stand-points. The writer Qian Zhongshu expressed one of them more than six decades ago. 'Only a fool cries "Hypocrite!" when immoral people start sermonising. I say hypocritical moralising is much more precious than honesty. When a morally upstanding person starts preaching that is nothing special, but when someone who has no moral principles wants to improve others, that shows real talent ... ' The only catch here is that the preacher's amorality should not be all too obvious to his audience.

Lao-tzu, the founder of Taoist philosophy, took another tack. Even 2,500 years ago he was fed up with the Confucians' continual moralising. 'Give up sainthood, renounce wisdom, and it will be a hundred times better for everyone. Give up kindness, renounce morality, and men will rediscover filial piety and love. Give up ingeniuity, renounce profit, and bandits and thieves will disappear,' he wrote in the *Tao Te Ching*. Lao-tzu's anarchic and not unappealing utopia goes so far as to say 'The best ruler is the one who is invisible to the people.'

Unfortunately the Taoists' political influence never reached far beyond the caves and valleys in which they led their hermits' lives. Thus China today is still a country where the citizens have no right to wish anything of the state, but the state has not only the right, but a duty, to mould its citizens as it wishes.

乱 **Luan**

Chaos

1. A structural deficit of Chinese football that has cost the country World Cup qualification for half a century.
2. The Chinese people's biggest nightmare. A government is good as long as it provides peace and harmony. Yet in China periods of relative calm have always been followed by times of great chaos (*da luan*) in which the populace has been brutally decimated. The Communist Party relies on this fear when it sprinkles a hint of *luan* into concepts such as pluralism and freedom of the press, while simultaneously chanting the old song of stability (*wen ding*). In reality that means the eternal rule

of the Party. The irony being of course that it was the same Communist Party that plunged the land into chaos rarely seen before. It is also apparent that the Chinese fear *luan* much like someone in Alcoholics Anonymous fears the bottle – anarchy is in their blood. That makes them in general a much more lively and spontaneous bunch than the Japanese, whom the Chinese both admire and find rather eerie. It also adds to the country's general confusion, visible not least on the roads. Many Chinese seem to attract chaos like magnets. In other countries the departments for transport have lines painted in the middle of roads, in Beijing barriers are erected. It is the only way to keep the motorised anarchists on the correct side. Any adherent of the 'Chinese threat' theory so popular in the United States should spend a day on Beijing's roads: the Chinese are still more a danger to themselves than to anyone else.

公德 Gongde

Good citizenship
Or: A nation of group egoists

Chinese intellectuals wring their hands when they think about how one morality campaign after another seems to stick with the public as well as water on a duck's back. They have come up with a wide variety of explanations. Some blame the Cultural Revolution for having destroyed old Chinese values. Others cite the 19th-century reformer Liang Qichao, who said that what the Chinese most regrettably lack is a sense of community. 'We need real education, it must take root in the people,' a Beijing filmmaker says. 'Not just this sham obedience that we observe now. Once the campaign is over, everything goes right back to the way it was before.' The often-discussed lack of community spirit is an interesting phenomenon. Someone who spits in the park would not spit in his own hallway. Chinese flats, even in dusty Beijing, are generally so spotlessly clean that every German hausfrau would go pale with envy. At the same time most Chinese do not have a problem with throwing their empty lunch-box out of the train window after their meal. And if they put it in the rubbish bag the inspector brings round, he'll just throw the whole bag out into the fields.

The Chinese like to think of themselves as unselfish, compared to the supposedly egotistical Westerners. Yet not even their own sayings bear this out. 'A Chinese on his own is like a dragon', but 'Put ten Chinese together and they are like a sack of fleas'. What a love of the collective! The Chinese sometimes envy the Japanese. They would like to be as disciplined and united in their efforts. Imagine 1.3 billion people marching in step. What they could achieve! Unfortunately already 13 Chinese have real difficulty acting in concert. Which is in its way likeable. In China the supposed trait of selflessness and self-

187

sacrifice tends to only cater to the *zi ji ren*, 'your own people', above all your family and your network of friends. The Chinese like to draw circles, dividing the world into 'inside' and 'outside'. They are group egoists, ready to do anything for their own people, but not interested in what happens outside the circle. They take the idea of 'loving your neighbour' rather literally, and of course they love their own family more than anyone else. The German sinologist Wolfgang Bauer once thought of this as an example where the West could learn from China. After all, a person who is asked to love the whole world, as Christians are, is soon overwhelmed by the task. It is easier for people to give warmth and affection if they can focus on loving those around them. Indeed, China does often seem more friendly and warm-hearted than Europe. Foreigners should not forget, however, that the Chinese have a tendency to be xenophiles. Westerners in particular may experience receptions much for friendly than those the Chinese would have in store for their own compatriots. The other side of the warm-heartedness between friends and relatives is the indifference to strangers. At the scene of an accident everyone rubbernecks but no one helps. A week does not go by without the media seizing on such an incident and experts despairingly discussing the lack of good citizenship.

One thing they never discuss though is the state's role in this. The Chinese are 'like a bowl of loose sand', Sun Yat-sen, the father of the 1911 democratic revolution, once famously said. 'They are millions of grains without anything to hold them together.' I for one suspect that it is not the inability of Chinese society to organise itself that demanded and led to a strong state. Rather, it is the Chinese state that by design keeps its society crippled. 'A weak people means a strong state, a strong people means the fall of the state,' it says in *The Book of Lord Shang*, a classic of the Legalist School. It was this school that gave China's First Emperor a philosophy to rule by over 2,200 years ago: 'Well governed states therefore do all they can to weaken the people ... A weak people obeys laws, an uncontrolled people becomes overly obstinate.' Mao Zedong held no emperor in higher esteem than the first one.

Mao's policy of keeping the people ignorant is a continuation of this pattern. For several years he ground into the dust anything that had a whiff of intelligence. The Chinese historian Sun Longji, who lives in the United States, talks about the historical 'infantilization' of Chinese adults. Not only was an emperor to 'love his people like his children', he should also treat them as such.

The patriarchs try to 'straighten up' the people, as the classics put it, and they accompany their sermons with threats of punishment. (China's Ministry of Justice was called the 'Ministry of Punishment' for two millennia.) Every attempt that society makes to organise itself is seen as a threat. This explains the merciless persecution of the Falun Gong sect and the often hysterical reaction of the authorities to environmental groups that spring up without government permission. Idealism is dangerous. Any communal gathering that is not exclusively concerned with satisfying physical needs (eating, sport) is suspect. Officials will be equally suspicious of a rock concert as of a voluntary support group of Aids patients. People acting in the right way often do it more out of a fear of punishment or gossip than out of moral conviction or inner principles. Not coincidentally, one of the Chinese signs for 'character', *pin*, consists of three mouths: 品.

However there is a impending danger for such a society if the corset that holds it together is suddenly removed, as happened during the catastrophic Cultural Revolution (1966–76). At that time Mao and his inquisitors incited children against their parents, schoolchildren against their teachers and husbands against their wives. A whole nation denounced itself year after year. Those who had been nearest and dearest were suddenly spitting in each other's faces, and often sending each other to their deaths. One teacher wrote a love poem to his wife. She turned him in and he was sent to a labour camp in Ningxia's desert for three years. And this example was no exception. 'People take serious things as a joke now, and crazy talk they take for real,' Zhang Xianliang writes in his novel *Half of Man Is Woman*, a book that holds a frightening mirror to the era. Such a traumatic experience is not easy for a nation to come to terms with. On the surface it may seem as though the scars have healed, but under the skin they still hurt. The Cultural Revolution has had a lasting effect on the way the Chinese live together. 'The legacy of that is going to cripple us for a long long time,' wrote Zhang Xianliang. The people who were young then are in their forties and fifties now. In their blood they still carry that era's poison: a deep mistrust. Even today the government does not permit a thorough, public debate on those times. 'No one trusts anyone else,' says a 38-year-old TV producer from Beijing. A Taiwanese lawyer who often works in China tells me that in her impression 'absolute egoism' is the rule at the moment, where people demonstrate community spirit often just for show. 'Many of my business partners wouldn't even hesitate to hurt the interests of their own family if they could turn a profit.' Their newfound prosperity hides the disorientation of China's people. If the emperor is the pole star around whom everyone finds their place, if the charisma of his virtue, *de*, alone can bring order to the empire, then what happens when he is lacking in virtue? What happens when the officials of the glorious Communist Party, once considered paragons of selflessness, self-sacrifice and dedication, have made a quite different reputation for themselves? When they are known to become rich through embezzlement and corruption, when they privatise the wealth of the nation into their own bank accounts?

That is when many normal Chinese start to think, 'Well, if you up there can steal four million, I'll steal my 400. I'd be silly not to!' That at least is what 74-year-old Kong Deyong thinks is happening. Kong Deyong is a 77th generation descendant of Confucius, but above all he is someone who has earned his money in Hong Kong through hard work. 'China today is a big piece of wood being gnawed on by millions of ants. It'll never get healthy like that,' he sighed. We were standing in the courtyard in front of his family's mansion in the pretty little town of Qufu. Businessman Kong Deyong was the last in his family to live in this palace before the Japanese invaded. He won't have anything to do with the old school's moral standards though. Kong is a charming lover of the good things in life, having nothing in common with the small group of neo-Confucianists who want to prescribe old remedies for a new China desperately trying to find its way. He has even less in common with the Communists. They mistreated him and put him in a labour camp for years because of his ancestor's famous name. 'Public morality is in trouble,' he said. That morning the newspaper had reported yet another disturbing case. A nursery director had put rat poison in the food of a competing nursery because its own business was not doing well. 'Mao clubbed to death Buddha, Lao-tzu and Confucius. Now he's dead. And we don't believe in Jesus,' said Kong Deyong. 'So what's left for us?'

China's cities now boast skyscrapers, the internet and MTV. But give the façade a tap, and you will hear it rings hollow. Something is brewing that has not yet found expression – a longing, a hunger. There remain gaping holes and unanswered questions that are twice as old as the Republic, and in the search for answers it did not help that the Communists have banned thought for five decades, and sometimes emotions and hope too. Guangzhou's glossy *New Weekly* put a woodcut of Lu Xun on the cover recently. 'Everything that we might curse today,' read the headline, 'Lu Xun has already cursed.' There is certainly something tragic about it. After the emperors, a republic, a civil war, a communist experiment and tens of millions of deaths, the same questions still hang in the air. They can be ignored, or misinterpreted, decorated with political slogans one day and jazzed up with glittering advertising posters the next, you can get high on the great utopias or on change and profit – these questions won't go away. They are questions relating to the very nature of this nation, and China is not one step closer to answering them. They go to the roots of corruption and the abuse of power. They reveal self-delusion and a search for identity. They speak of megalomania as well as an inferiority complex. How should China deal with a world that has forced itself upon it, and that it won't be able to spirit away? And then the old question reappears: how should the Chinese act towards each other? The clear-sighted Lu Xun called it a 'cannibal culture', nothing more than a feast of human flesh that the rich and powerful have prepared for themselves. He castigated his people for their 'slave mentality'. 'How easily we let ourselves be enslaved,' wrote Lu Xun, 'and how extremely happy we are with it.' Yes, he admitted bitterly, now and then a flicker of hope stirs in the Chinese – the hope of 'enslaving or eating others, and so to forget that they themselves are enslaved and will be eaten.' He only had one thing left to say in the end: 'Save the children.'

If they are not long dead and buried like Lu Xun, those children are now very old people. In the little bit of daylight still allotted to them, they can see a China where there have perhaps never been so many niches as there are now. In these little spaces of freedom people can do whatever they want to do. And are they happy? Much has changed, while some things remain as they were. The majority of people, however, still live in the same pecking order Lu Xun has described. You still meet people like the young engineer I bumped into in a hotel in Guangxi. He worked for a large state company. 'You want to be a human being when the others are animals?' he said. 'You can try. But you'll end up on the losing side.'

有事 **You shi**

To have something to do

What do you have to do? No one will ask. Wherever you are in China you can murmur a *'you shi'* to excuse yourself painlessly from any situation. Whether for the business acquaintance creeping out of a conference, or for the diner making his excuses before the dessert, *you shi* is a magic formula that has to be unquestioningly accepted due to a 5,000-year-old cultural understanding. Excuses thus become wonderfully practical in China. No probing questions like in Europe ('Oh yes?', 'What are you up to?', 'Where are you going?'), no tortuous efforts to wriggle out of answering them, no embarrassed blushing. In China you are not forced to justify yourself and so there is no need to lie. Everybody has to show consideration for the other person's 'face'. That guarantees a harmonious goodbye. In the end it is a mark of respect for the other person's free will. One's decision to leave is accepted. Perhaps it is mentally filed away, but no song and dance is made of it. Of course, even the most convenient customs can be mixed blessings. I recently found myself in one of these exceptional situations on a trunk road out in the country. The only other vehicle was a lonely lorry rumbling down the middle of the road right in front of me. Suddenly, without a warning or any obvious reason, the lorry squealed to a stop – not on the right-hand side of the road, or on the verge, but right on the central dividing line. My car bumped into the back of it. I jumped out, ran up to the cab and started shouting at the driver: What was he playing at? What had he been thinking? Was he crazy? Idiot! etc. His laconic answer: '*You shi!*' Me: speechless.

宣传 *Xuan chuan*

Propaganda
Wine that is not wine

The ancient Taoist book *Jade Record* meticulously describes the many chambers and levels of hell. The Tower of Oblivion lies right underneath hell's 10th palace. The tower has ten rooms and in each room the demons lay out goblets of the 'wine that is not wine'. Newly-arrived souls are forced to drink their goblet to the dregs. Only then will the place, time and form of their reincarnation be decided. The drink erases all memory of their previous life. Then they are thrown into the river of hell, which carries them along to the base of a red wall. An inscription on the wall reads 'It is easy to be a human. It is hard to live a human life. To desire to be a human the second time is even harder.' Two demons then haul the souls onto dry land and set them into their allotted places in their new lives. One demon is called 'Life is short', the other 'Death has stages'.

With the army's butchering of the peaceful 1989 demonstrators still fresh in his mind, the young union leader Han Dongfang wrote the following: 'To anyone who can hear me, remember what I am saying. I don't want to be a Chinese in my next life. Don't be a Chinese. Being Chinese is too terrible, too sad.' It is true that these lines arose during a time of extreme tumult and unhappiness, and yet they are part of a current that penetrates much of Chinese consciousness. This nation never had much to laugh about. Even today, when a modest prosperity has established itself in the cities, it is easy to get the impression that many Chinese see life first of all as a matter of suffering and testing. The word for happiness is *kuai le*, the fleeting joy. Naturally poets of almost every culture have sung of the short-lived nature of happiness, and the French measure their *bonheur* by the hour, yet one still gets the feeling that in China happiness is a particularly rare and fleeting treasure. You only need to turn the television on or go to the cinema to notice the two main traits of Chinese actors: their infinite capacity for pathos and an even greater supply of tears. Traditionally Chinese books and films end with a heart-breaking separation. Or the protagonists simply pass away. Viewers can count themselves lucky if only one of the main characters has hanged or shot himself by the end. The American happy ending never found many fans among China's literati and scriptwriters.

So imagine what a thoroughly melancholy affair the printed word and the flickering screen would be in China without the benevolence of the Communist Party. It was this party that decided that a happy people is as much a part of socialism as the mole is part of Mao's chin. And indeed, since the Communists came to power happiness has become a staple ingredient on the front pages of all newspapers. Maybe it is their idea of psychotherapy. So the caring rulers wield the power of suggestion via countless variations on the eternal headline: 'Tomorrow everything will be *even* better.' Even those whose last hour has come cannot complain. 'Two farmers from Yunnan province convicted for drug trafficking benefited from the latest advances in China's judicial system,' began a full-page article in *Beijing Today*. 'Instead of facing a firing squad, they were executed by lethal injection … This is evidence that China's death penalty is becoming ever more civilised and humane.'

Just as the farmers from Yunnan are delighted with their right to lethal injections, so are the Tibetans rejoicing in the railway line to Lhasa that daring Chinese engineers have laid over permafrost and deep gorges. But does their bliss match that of the television viewers who were treated to a musical ode to this monumental project? One of the state broadcaster's gala evenings had a choir of railwaymen singing about it. The men were all in their forties and wore overalls, wellies and construction helmets – all bright yellow. The boiler-suit ballet consti- tutes its own artistic genre on Chinese television. In evening programmes dancing proletarians take their place next to a tutu-ed police force and soldiers in ballet tights. The police and the People's Liberation Army both have their own choirs and ballet troupes, from whose ranks Mao Zedong used to recruit women comrades for sexual pleasures. The yellow railway-men began their show by teasingly lifting their right yellow wellies as if on stage at the Moulin Rouge, just a little more rheumatically. All the while they sang, believe it or not, 'Da-da-day, da-da-day, Tibet will get its own railway'. Then they danced a railwayman's polka. In slow motion of course: the hard work, the permafrost, you know. Let me assure you that this was not meant as a cabaret performance, but as a solemn hymn to the spirit of self-sacrifice of the workers and engineers who do their utmost for the indestructible unity of the Chinese peoples. I enjoyed watching it. It made a nice change from the Liberation Army's tenors and sopranos, all decorated with medals, who normally round out the programme. These singing Christmas trees usually stand proudly in front of a video wall. While the viewer can watch jet fighters taking off behind them, from under heroically raised eyebrows they gaze out into the distance as they howl like strangled cats about their sweet love for the country, for which they would give body and soul. Now that would be worth seeing. Would they be able to cause as much damage to enemy troops as to the poor folks on their sofas on the home front?

Not only has socialism introduced happy endings to China, it likes them so much that it shares them generously with film-makers, who somehow do not manage to come up with the idea. The popular Hong Kong action film *Infernal Affairs* from 2002 is a good example. The story is about the rivalry between a cop who turns out to be a mafia mole and a gangster who in fact is an honest undercover agent. Two versions were filmed: in the Hong Kong original the baddie wins out, but in China's cinemas it is the – well, the one that always wins in fairyland.

The Communist Party's propaganda often is so obviously absurd and indigestible, that it would be easy just to dismiss it with a laugh. After all, there is a new China now, isn't there? People drink coffee in Starbucks and surf the net wirelessly at the same time. Young people care more for sex, food, money and consumerism than for politics. But it is not that cut and dried. It is still amazing to observe the power that the Party's thinking and its slogans exert, even on people who are openly critical of the Party or even cynical about it. It is a fact that no one believes in Communism any more. But try to have a discussion about Tibet or Taiwan with the young businessman whom just a second ago you found intelligent, witty and open-minded, and you will see what I mean. Propaganda does work. Even now. That can be a sobering discovery. Oscar Wilde once said that beliefs were not accepted because they are sensible, but because they are repeated. Perhaps people are that simple.

People are of course aware that their government is bent on leaving them in the dark about many things. That the main objective of China's media – which on the surface today gives an appearance of colour and diversity – is not to inform them. This only makes the hunger for information all the stronger – it is a hunger that grows ravenous in times of crisis. Exactly the times when the rulers manage the flow of information even more strictly, for fear of losing control. This makes for ideal breeding conditions for a popular folk medium: the rumour.

China now is the country with more mobile phone users than any other on the globe, while it is only second to the United States in the number of internet users. During the last big crisis, the outbreak of the SARS virus, mobile phones and the internet did indeed play a major role. But it was not the role they might have had in other countries where they would have been instruments for spreading of the latest news. The censors didn't allow that in China. Instead, e-mails and text messages ensured that a tidal wave of rumours of a magnitude never before seen swept across the country. Text messages were the principal carriers of these *xiao dao xiao xi*, 'little path news' as they are called here. 'Don't go outside tonight!' one message warned me early in the epidemic. 'Air force planes will be flying over Beijing, spraying poisonous chemicals.'

A fascinating two-page story in the Guangzhou newspaper *Southern Weekend* traced the route of a rumour that had spread over 14 provinces in only four days, undergoing the most varied of metamorphoses on the way. The most common version of it went: 'Have you heard? A baby was born in XY that could already speak. Set off fireworks and drink green bean soup, the baby said. That will keep away the SARS virus! After uttering these words the child died.' Through whatever towns the rumour passed, crowds gathered and let off fireworks. Beans quickly sold out. But just as the people feared the virus, their government feared the rumours. Dozens of 'irresponsible rumourmongers' were tracked down by the police and arrested. Some were later sentenced to years of imprisonment. What is particularly interesting about the baby legend is that it goes back several centuries in almost the same form. The *Southern Weekend* report seems interesting for another reason too. The report (based almost entirely on police sources) traces the rumour's route down a chain of conversations and text messages of normal people who had never before acted out of the ordinary. Yet these conversations were all reported in detail, down to the minute: 'On the evening of 5 May, 9:31pm, Ms. Kong from Wenquan district in Hubei province said in a phone call: I've heard that a woman in the Xian'andan Mountain region gave birth to a baby ... ' The report gave an inadvertent insight into the extent of everyday surveillance in China.

The main role of propaganda in China today is to gradually lead people to forget that the Party has left the communist utopia (its actual *raison d'être*) behind a long time ago. It aims to prevent the Party from the fate of the naked emperor in the famous fairytale where only a small child finds the courage to exclaim 'But he isn't wearing any clothes', and so breaks the spell of fear that had held sway over the people until then. It is not communism that rules in China now, it is just naked power. Yes, there are political changes, but they are not always those hoped for by the West. The regime is in fact shedding its very skin: a left-wing dictatorship is in the process of turning into a right-wing one. The consequences are both impressive (prosperity in the cities, the retreat of ideology) and frustrating (the self-enrichment of the elite, the lack of rights of workers and farmers). The colour of power has changed. Due to the widening gap between rich and poor, some commentators have begun to speak of a 'Latin-Americanisation' of China. The Party leadership calls it 'socialism with Chinese characteristics'. While on the look-out for a new justification of its existence, the formulaic references to the old spirits serve a twofold purpose: firstly to placate those in the country who are still sentimental about the old days, and secondly – not unlike a slow fade in a film – to gradually make the Party's origins vanish and have them replaced with new images and slogans. The rulers hope that they can win over their subjects through their stomachs: with a continual increase in affluence. On the one hand you can see it as an encouraging sign of progress that this state and this Party actually feel the need, the duty even, to justify itself now. On the other hand it is somewhat disconcerting to observe how the rulers use Chinese nationalism as the new opiate of the masses, particularly for young Chinese.

The equation is very simple. It goes like this: we

are making China great and strong. Anyone who is against us does not love his country. The *People's Daily's* most popular online service currently is the Strong Nation Forum. There you will mostly find, according to its webmaster, 30-to-40-year-olds railing against Japan and America. It is particularly the anger against Japan that the Party consciously manipulates and cultivates. It has its roots in the Japanese war crimes against China which Japan has still not adequately recognised and for which it has not yet apologised. Not that this stops the Party having an excellent working relationship with Japanese investors. Blind nationalism is not a flame that can be fanned without consequences however, and it is not impossible that China's rulers will find themselves in the same position as the sorceror's apprentice in the Goethe poem who loses control of his brooms. Some already feel called upon to take matters into their own hands. In autumn 2003 Japanese exchange students were performing a sketch at Northwest University in Xi'an. They wore red bras over their T-shirts and pulled bits of paper out of them that they scattered over the audience.

As the Japanese later said, the sketch was supposed to end with a declaration of friendship with China: the backs of their T-shirts carried the phrases 'Japan loves China' and 'China loves Japan'. They just never got that far. The outraged audience interrupted their performance. Soon the rumour was going round that *ri ben gui zi*, Japanese devils, had been making fun of China. A mob of thousands of students roamed the campus to root out any Japanese. Afterwards they marched into the city and besieged Japanese restaurants there. Anti-Japanese riots on a far larger scale shook Shanghai and Hangzhou in 2005. China's schools, universities and mass media still teach the country's recent history as one long series of humiliations (*guo chi*). The only one to show a way out of this endless spiral of shame and disgrace is the wise leadership of the Party. On the one hand you have the continual parroting of China's humiliations at the hands of foreign powers over the last century and a half, on the other hand since Mao's death you have a glorification of China's own cultural heritage – in fact of the exact same things and thoughts that under

Mao were ruthlessly being smashed and meant to be exterminated. The country once again is taking refuge in the assertion that it always had been superior to everyone else. And in fact, still is. The unspoken inference here is that the rest of the world will soon recognise exactly that.

A part of this ritual is the patriots' sometimes amusing, but mostly tiresome insistence on proving that the Chinese were always first at everything. Football and golf they have already reclaimed as achievements of Chinese culture. Soon they will no doubt dig up a Han-era snowboard in Xi'an. And when the Chang E spacecraft one day really does reach the moon, it will beam pictures back to earth of the star-loving Ming official Wan Hu, who shot himself into space on a chair powered by bamboo rockets. Wan Hu will be sitting there on live TV, drinking his 600-year-old Coca Cola and telling his tale of how in 1969 he welcomed a certain Neil Armstrong and congratulated him on being the second man to set foot on the moon.

The further China's history can be stretched back

in time the more fruitfully it can be exploited. Until the Communist Revolution, China's scholars would always refer to China's 3,000-year history. In less than 50 years the Communist Party succeeded in adding two whole millennia to that claim. (Although the Nazi Party topped even that: establishing and sinking a Thousand Year Reich in just 12 years.) Nowadays it is almost impossible to hear a speech in which the speaker does not respectfully mention those hallowed '5,000 years'. The speakers now even have the pseudo-science with which to back up their claims. Working enormously hard, archaeologists and historians employed by the government have managed to discover just what the government already knew. Fancy that! China now officially has over '5,000 years of gardening culture' that it can invoke, as well as '5,000 years of sport'. Both of these quotes are taken from recent newspaper articles. It goes without saying that the trademarks of Chinese culture – tea, silk and Jackie Chan – can be dated to the same era, although Jackie Chan's earlier kung fu films have since rightly been forgotten.

Some 5,000-years of history is a cause of great pride, but it can also be a great burden. A business partner might mention it with a sigh, holding it responsible for the nation's lack of innovation and flexibility. That need not be the case though, as the Communists now prove. After all, they made the people 'the rulers of the land for the first time in 5,000 years'. They also brought China 'its first Olympic Games in 5,000 years'. Nor do the Taiwanese want to be caught napping. They claim to have held 'the first free elections in 5,000 years', although they have yet to provide archaeological evidence. The US boxing promoter Don King early in the new millennium even promised to give the Chinese 'the first heavyweight world championship fight in the great People's Republic's 5,000-year history'. He himself came, and historians and aerodynamicists quickly agreed that such a shock of hair had never entered Chinese airspace before. In the end he gave China a cancelled heavyweight world championship fight. Quite an event: the first of its kind in 5,000 years.

国花 **Guo hua**

The national flower

Is the peony, most Chinese think. Except, it is not. China does not have a national flower, at least no officially-recognised one. This is a disgrace, if we are to believe Professor Chen Junyu who has triggered a debate on this subject. Professor Chen claims that China is 'the only great nation without a national flower'. He is pressing for an end to this 'chaotic situation' in which now the peony and now the plum blossom is gaining upper hand among the Chinese. The peony was the favourite flower of many of the emperors: it stands for wealth and nobility; in poems it symbolises a young woman, and when 'dew drops on the peony', even more so. Its rival the plum flowers in cold winter months and so became a poetic embodiment of the toughness of the Chinese. One frustrated chat-room user found the debate itself rather symbolic: 'The fact that we've been discussing this for dozens of years without getting anywhere is so typically Chinese.' There were a good many cynical reactions to the debate. 'So what if our flower is ten times more beautiful than America's? Is it going to feed us?' someone asked in the internet. Someone else called it an 'idiot's dream', while another suggested the 'naming of a national hen'. America, by the way, has chosen the rose as its national flower, while the state of Texas even managed to name a state vegetable: the onion. Whether this says anything about affinities between Texas and Wales, associated as it is with the leek, I wouldn't like to hazard a guess.

假 *Jia*

All fake
The People's Republic of Cheats

An e-mail was going round among young people in Shanghai and Beijing not long ago. The subject line was 'Why those of us born in the seventies are in a fix'. 'When we were small, we were taught to be good children,' the e-mail began. 'But since we've become grown-ups, we've only had fake brand cigarettes to smoke, fake brand wine to drink and hypocritical words to speak. We get duped by people with faked qualifications and we sign fake receipts. The worst thing is: even the football games we watch are fixed.' Even before the Hong Kong *Far Eastern Economic Review* suggested that the letters PRC stood for 'People's Republic of Cheats', foreigners were just as uncomfortable with the situation as young Chinese were. 'The Chinese are very ingenious at imitation', an impressed traveller from Portugal wrote. 'They have imitated to perfection whatsoever they have seen brought out of Europe. In the province of Canton they have counterfeited several things so exactly, that they sell them inland for goods brought out from Europe.' The traveller's name was Domingo Navarette. He was a Dominican priest and journeyed through China between 1659 and 1664. In other words, the accusations are not new – yet perhaps they were never voiced as vociferously as they are today. It is hard to think of a word that pops up as often in discussions with Chinese intellectuals and artists as *jia*. *Jia* refers to duplicity in all its many shades: it can mean something counterfeit, faked, copied, it can mean hypocrisy or a sham. The 'Fake' is one of this country's leitmotifs, like its much admired growth and its unflustered spirit of change. It is one of the constants in this place of turbulent upheavals. Everything grows, everything flows, nothing is what it seems. China – country of unlimited opportunities, kingdom of barefaced pirates and counterfeiters.

There are two principal reasons why this has become more serious recently: one is the globalisation of trade, the other the country's political structure. Modernity on the one hand and an anachronism on the other, in particular the curious co-existence of the two is responsible. This overlap can seem rather strange to a European schooled in logic and clarity. Admittedly in China the past and the future do bare their teeth at each other sometimes, but you can find them just as often cuddled cosily together. Sometimes the absurd comedy of the situation leaps out at you, sometimes it calls for a clear-eyed observer.

In the West we know all about pirate Goretex anoraks, Rolexes and *Lord of the Rings* DVDs – after all, we are often actors in this play, both unwittingly and willingly. The European Union reported in 2003 that 87 million faked products had been seized in that year – almost nine times as many as just five years before. Almost two-thirds of them came from China, not least because China has become the world's workshop, taking delivery of the blueprints for the authentic products. The trainers the purchasing agents from Nike order leave via the front door. Meanwhile the traders from Yaxiu Market are waiting at the back door. This heaven for pirated copies is as popular with tourists as it is with diplomats' spouses. Sometimes you can meet a real foreign minister in the market. Italy's Franco Frattini was caught there by journalists one fine October morning in the act of buying a fake Rolex. What was the minister doing in Beijing? He had come for EU-China summit. Topping the agenda of the summit was China's lack of respect for intellectual property rights.

There is scarcely a product that inventive Chinese producers would not copy, be it golf clubs or the White House (a newly-rich farmer in Hangzhou had that one built for himself). Although it is certainly true that the intellectual effort behind the originals is a valuable commodity, one positive aspect of the copying is little discussed; namely the fact that the criminal activities of some counterfeiters are as beneficial to China as any development aid. The fact is that sometimes stolen intellect can be a blessing too. The US industry's International Intellectual Property Alliance estimates that China's illegal copies of films, software and books cause $2.6 billion of damage to the industry every year. Practically every Chinese computer runs on pirated software and everyone who watches a DVD buys the pirate copy for six to ten yuan (or the really great copies for 20 yuan). Looking at it another way though, if only the originals could be bought, the overwhelming majority of today's Chinese would have to go without. 'Copies meant that I could catch up on the West's pop culture, starting with the Beatles,' a musician friend of mine tells me. 'And I've seen all of Fassbinder's and Fellini's films.' Copying at the moment is probably the most powerful and sustainable method of introducing China's masses to Western culture, thus making no humble contribution to cross-cultural understanding. Yes, it is at the expense of the Western cultural industries, but not entirely without the approval of some of the industry players. 'The more people who see a film, the better', said the director Michael Winterbottom when he was asked in Beijing what he thought of pirate copies of his films.

Naturally a desire for easy money drives the market in copies. Yet some of the brand scroungers spice up their creations with their own creativity. There are the fusion copyists. Take, for example, the fast-food chain who synthesised its American role models by calling itself 'McKentucky' (*Mai Kenji* in Chinese). Then there is the car producer Geeli. Even they seem to have found their old model a little too daring. Not only did it have a radiator grille copied from Mercedes, it also prominently featured the Mercedes star on the bonnet. The new model's design now combines the Mercedes grille with a logo based on BMW's. Another original invention that sprang from the addiction to brand names is the 'Armani' shirt that will be sold with a 'Boss' price-tag in a 'Ralph Lauren' box. Apart from the fusion artists, there are simple con men who palm off their own wares under famous names. While the rest of the world was eagerly awaiting the publication of the sixth Harry Potter volume, *Harry Potter and the Half-Blood Prince*, readers in China already had

a dozen Harry Potter adventures to choose from —
including *Harry Potter and the Golden Turtle* and *Harry
Potter and the Leopard Dragon*. They gave away their
Chinese origin though , not least in one of the book's
'sweet and sour shower' in which Harry gets caught.
The young bestselling author and racing driver Han
Han, famous for his devastating reckoning with the
Chinese school system, told me that he has already
collected over 20 different novels that have appeared
under his name. 'If one of my books is illegally copied
and sold, I couldn't care less — but to write a dreadful
novel and then put my name to it, that's a slur.'

Indeed, there is a serious side to the issue. The
insipid Chinese truffles (*Tuber indicum*) may only cause
a shock of disappointment and righteous indignation on a French palate craving the *Tuber melanospo-
rum*. Other fakes can be a danger to life and limb.
Fake Nokia phone batteries explode in Chinese ears
and fake brand cigarettes between Chinese lips. Fake
medicines kill 200,000 Chinese every year, say official
reports.

And the less tangible consequences? China's society

suffers as much as the coffers of big companies. The *China Daily* reported that millions of Chinese children learn from cheaply imitated textbooks which contain a multitude of wrongly written characters. Badly educated? Didn't get into university? Don't worry, a well faked university degree costs just 200 yuan (£15) in Beijing. Scarcely a week goes by without mobile phone users receiving text messages advertising 'all kinds of references, receipts and official stamps'. More than half a million faked Masters and PhDs are in circulation, two-thirds of all state companies cook their books, and tens of thousands of official statistics are made up each year. You may or may not believe these figures – they are all official statistics from the government, a government in fact, which itself must take a considerable portion of the blame for the country's reputation. In this bad apple the worm is nestling right in the core.

More than once the state-run media have announced national campaigns like the one to bring to account those high-ranking Party and government officials who have faked degrees. The problem has apparently reached pandemic proportions. The *People's Daily* put this down as a 'scandalous con': 'If a high ranking official resorts to deception and fraud, couldn't the same official also pull the wool over our eyes as he goes about implementing the Party's guidelines and policies?' That is certainly a valid conclusion – but one that still needs to be taken a step further. As a Chinese proverb puts it, 'If the ridge beam is crooked, all the other beams will be crooked too.' Meaning: if the biggest con men are occupying the seats in the Central Committee in Beijing, who can blame the common people and lowly officials who only follow the example of the top dogs?

The regime's most elaborate masquerade is this: it simulates socialism where in reality naked power reigns. Many foreigners have realised by now that the communism so insistently trumpeted by China's leaders is simply a sham to bluff their own people. What they have not realised is, that the opposite assumption – strongly promoted by clever investment agencies in China – is not true either: the country has not plumped yet for Western-style capitalism. Yes, the Chinese are passionate businesspeople, but to call the playing field in today's China a 'market economy' would be a gross deception. In today's China the common currency most often is not ideas, hard work and entrepreneurial initiative. It is political power that is exchanged for economic advantage. Observers of China have talked of 'cadre capitalism'. Contacts and bribes oil the system, not the free market. Yet where political patrons have allowed it, the most wild and untamed capitalism flourishes. Lenin is said to have once remarked, the farther east that capitalism reaches, the more brazen it becomes. Partly this game of pretence is a matter of pragmatism. The Party sees it as a convenient way to drag the stubborn remnants of the old society into the new times. These are the people who still hold Mao and Marx dear and could easily obstruct the path of progress. Deception for the sake of the Party's prestige is quite another matter. When the Olympic Committee's inspectors paid the city a visit, armies of day labourers were engaged to spray the unsightly brown grass along Beijing's main roads green. Similarly, one of the Olympic posters promised in Chinese characters 'A new century, a new Beijing', while the English translation read 'A new century, an ancient Peking'. That was the version aimed at nostalgic foreigners. Mostly the lying serves one purpose: to maintain the Party's power. To that end language itself is taken hostage, words are falsified. Chinese television: it's one shrill false tone. When the officials talk of 'news', they mean propaganda, when they talk of 'the people' they mean themselves. 'Stability' refers to their eternal rule and concepts that they have enjoyed using in the last few years such as 'human rights', 'the rule of law' and 'democracy' are to be understood in relation to mainly one end: the nation's 'stability'.

Power was once about control, now it is just as much about money. In the process it has lost its sovereign charisma, the imperial virtue that the Confucians once evoked. In earlier times the Party was able to shackle its subjects in a tight ideological corset. Later that ideology may have proved itself crazy, even murderous, but at the time it provoked religious belief. Some of its basic values provided moral guidance – the spartan lifestyle, the sacrifices for the collective, the rejection of profit. Today, people don't trust the authorities. They see through the facade, they recognise the lies and the corruption. They still look to their leaders for stability, for peace and for the dividends of prosperity, but apart from that, government officials are believed to only use all those empty words to mask their greed for personal gain. The old values have been thrown overboard, new ones are yet to be taken on. So is it any surprise that the rank and file imitate their masters? That the whole country is awash with copies, shams and sleight of hand? For fun and for the cash, some Westerners who live in China have invented a second life for themselves as 'foreigners for hire'. When they get the call from a Chinese company or organisation, they slip into a suit and tie. On one day they jump onto the stage as a 'foreign investor' and sign contracts as flashbulbs pop. The next day they add a touch of glamour and authenticity to solemn official events. Nor is this just a provincial custom. A German sinology student once appeared at an environmental conference in Beijing's

Great Hall of the People as a 'foreign expert', and lectured 2,000 dignitaries on the achievements of Chinese environmental policy. The same student earns more pocket money from a Beijing architectural practice. He is their original German architect, this time with a cashmere scarf thrown over his shoulders. His Chinese bosses pay him 1,000 yuan for each performance, making it quite clear that he should on no account let on that he speaks fluent Chinese. 'Here it's always better to be foreign,' says the student by way of explanation. 'As a foreigner you are the trophy they have bagged.'

Most of the time though the Chinese themselves are the actors. In the little town of Yangshuo in Guangxi province you can see an awe-inspiring 1,000-year-old banyan tree. The tree's dignity is in stark contrast to the theme park which the local government has built around it in order to charge entry. And this in a place that was a natural paradise before. It is set beside a dreamily meandering river, beyond which clusters of giant bamboo hem the foot of the mountain. The entry ticket covers an all-singing, all-dancing show by ethnic minorities, a favourite with Chinese tourists. Every 10 minutes you can see Mulao women jumping between two bamboo poles that are being hit together rhythmically. After the show tourists can, for 10 yuan, have their photos taken with these exotic women clad in colourful costumes and turbans. Only, they are not really Mulao women. 'No, where did you get that idea? We're all Chinese women from around here,' a 17-year-old dancer told me. 'You know,' she said, 'the real Mulao can't speak Chinese properly. It's much more convenient for tourists like this.'

Parks with a minority or historical theme are springing up everywhere. They are just one example of a phenomenon that has swept the whole country: the disneyfication of China. It is the outcome of the terribly fertile symbiosis of three factors. Firstly, the desire for profit that currently grips China. Secondly, China's long-standing relaxed attitude towards historical originals. (China's temples and palaces were mainly built of wood. They regularly burnt down, and also weathered quickly. Therefore they were regularly replaced, yet they were still considered to be the original buildings: the spirit in which a building was erected and cared for was more important than the age of its building materials.) Yet these two factors could not have caused half as much damage if it were not for a third one, the historical amnesia that the rulers have imposed on their people for half a century now. The communist regime cannot survive without the regular shock of amnesia they induce to the collective and the forced short-term memory loss that results. Only thus will its crimes be forgotten and its lies appear less monstrous. Most importantly of all, it needs to conceal the patterns and mechanisms of power that are at the root of all the traumatic events of the recent past, from the Great Leap Forward and the Cultural Revolution to the massacre on Tiananmen Square.

More proof that the Chinese are not allowed a political or historical memory came with the propaganda fanfare following the SARS catastrophe. Had anyone managed to cast his or her mind back only two months (during all the preceding months the

231

government had hushed up and denied the epidemic), he or she would have shouted out 'Lies!' As it was, everyone agreed on the official formula that the amazing Communist Party had once again saved the country from certain destruction. The arsonist was praised for being a fireman. Was this publicly displayed loyalty a sham? Maybe, but that is just the point that the e-mail at the start of this chapter made: in a state like this hypocrisy becomes second nature to its citizens. When I asked China's rock star Cui Jian what annoyed him most about his country, he replied 'zhuang sha', the way everybody is acting the fool.

The mix of a carefree attitude towards tradition, a thirst for profit and the recurrent forced amnesia leaves its mark on cities too. Just look at the hopeless parody of an 'old town' in Shanghai, which in reality is all brand new. 'Traditional-style' houses have been blown up into monstrous travesties of 'the pictur-esque'. Similar caricatures are popping up all over the nation, from the holy centre of Lhasa to the environs of Beijing's Forbidden City where govern-ment swindlers are now destroying the last remaining heritage sites. Recently a model restoration project was announced for parts of Beijing's Nanchizi Street, where wonderful examples of *siheyuan*, old Peking's courtly mansions, could be found. At the end of the project there suddenly stood brand new, multi-storey townhouses with multiple garages for the Mercedes and Audis of the *nouveau riche*. 'Old town restoration' is the Chinese term for tearing down and reconstructing – bigger, 'more beautiful' and 'more practical' buildings. Today though there is one major difference to the ancestors' casual attitude to the substance of architecture: the respect for tradition has now disappeared, its venerable spirit has been banished. In its place the city elders now bank on real estate projects and a low-maintenance Disney-China that they can channel tourists through. Spooky.

A friend of mine who would dearly love to be a patriot and yet knows how hard that is in his country, shouted out once, 'Fake! Everything about this place is fake! Just one thing is for real: the trickery, that's real.' Of course this was a little exaggerated – China is full of honest and touchingly upright people. But what he said mirrors what they often feel – if you are honest, people take advantage of you.

There circulates a blackly comic anecdote in China. A poor farmer spends the last of his money buying a few sacks of seed. He sows them and waits – nothing grows, the seeds were fake. The despairing farmer does not want to live any longer. He goes into his shed and finds a bottle of rat poison. He drinks it all – nothing happens, the poison seller has tricked him. His family find him and are over the moon that he has survived the suicide attempt. They decide to celebrate and open a bottle of good rice wine. Now the farmer drops dead – it was counterfeit liquor, highly poisonous.

Confucius once said that anyone who wants to bring order to a state must first 'correct the names' or concepts. For 'if names be not correct, language is not in accordance with the truth of things, and affairs cannot be carried on to success. When affairs cannot be carried on to success, rites and music will not flourish. When rites and music do not flourish, punishment will not be properly awarded. When punishments are not properly awarded, the people do not know how to move hand or foot.' And so it is in China today. Things are not as they seem, and most people are at a loss as to how to move their hands and feet.

没有 *Mei you*

Don't have any

Is only included here for nostalgic reasons. Until a few years ago *mei you* was the first and often only Chinese phrase that every visitor to China knew. It was feared because it was the grumpy reply that you were greeted with from morning to night, whether in a department store, your hotel or at an airline's ticket desk. It generally passed through the unsmiling lips of a scruffy state employee, who would immediately let his head sink back onto his sleeve-protector, which apparently had been invented for the sole purpose of protecting his blue polyester jacket from the layer of dust on the counter as he napped. Tourists snapped up *mei you* T-shirts that canny street sellers had made. Today *mei you* is history. It went the way of the planned economy. China's shops and markets are today flooded with goods and the shopkeepers and sales assistants wave at you from a distance and pluck at your sleeve as you pass. They work on commission now. This change from a sellers' to a buyers' market has introduced a new phrase into the tourist vocabulary. Nowadays you're faced with hordes of postcard hawkers and knitwear toreros who, like red-cloaked bull-fighters throwing themselves before their four-legged opponents, will throw themselves and their crochet blankets in the way of tourists who are desperately trying to escape them. So now you can hear many tourists screaming *bu yao*, which translates as 'Don't want it. I don't want it! I REALLY DON'T WANT IT!'

劳模 *Lao mo*

Model workers
Serving the people

I can't really remember when the idea for this chapter hit me. Was it on that frosty December evening? When a waitress welcomed me with a wide smile, holding out a steaming hot terry towel that I lowered my head into so blissfully that I almost forgot all about eating? Was it in the teahouse in Chengdu? Where a skilful ear cleaner concentrated, as is the custom there, on digging the wax out of my and my friends' ears with a little bamboo spoon while we let the world drift by over a pot of Wulong tea? No, I believe it was the night that I landed at Beijing airport after three days of skiing and nursing chilblains. I stomped to my car, tired and exhausted, looking forward to my bed as I

turned the key in the ignition. Nothing happened
– I had left the lights on and the battery was dead. I
could have wept.

In Britain you would call the AA or RAC. What
do you do in China? You persuade a taxi driver to
tow you to the nearest village, where there are a row
of repair garages. It was midnight when we arrived,
it was pitch dark, everybody was asleep. No problem,
the taxi driver said, and hammered on a garage door.
Soon a man appeared in oil-stained pyjamas, his hair
uncombed. Two minutes later the lights went on and
three men rubbing the sleep out of their eyes surrounded my car, behind them their boss, a woman.
They replaced the battery in a jiffy, but then an
argument started – they did not have a starter cable
in the garage. Before long one of them had an idea.
He grabbed a wire cutter and ran across the street
to the peacefully slumbering garage opposite us. He
clambered up its outside wall and snipped off three
yards of a power cable that was dangling from the roof.
He returned beaming, holding out our starter cable.
Half an hour later I was home. I know that the robbed

neighbour might have his own opinion on the matter, but since that day I feel like shouting out to the world that China is a service paradise. I am running no little risk in saying this and I hesitated for a long time in writing this. One of my good friends even threatened to break off our friendship if I did – or, at least, to unmask me as a manipulative ignoramus. But then I sank my head once more into the pile of soft towels at the Cleopatra hair salon and slipped away from all the city's bustle. One reason that Cleopatra had become my regular hairdresser's was the bitter rivalry between the neighbourhood's German, French and Russian ladies as they fought for the favour of the good-looking hairdresser from China's northeast. It was amusing to watch the women waiting for their respective back-combing sessions woo the young man and his skilful hands. They blushed when his coal-black eyes met theirs in the mirror. The many Russian customers put themselves at an unfair advantage. Once their blond atomic mushrooms had been pumped up, they often shoved a bank note down the hairdresser's shirt. The more cheeky pushed theirs into the front pocket of his tight jeans, obviously needing to give the note a little helping hand until it was securely stowed away. (Our street, bordering the northern side of an embassy compound, has been so completely taken over by Russians that the rickshaw drivers will address any Westerner in Russian. Around the corner you will find the 'Russian market', where the clientele from Moscow and Novosibirsk load themselves up with piles of neon purple and bright blue fur coats and with bras so spacious that you could fit three Chinese women inside one cup.)

As I was saying, there I lay with my eyes closed while two firm hands kneaded me into a blissful trance. They drummed on my shoulders, scratched my scalp, boxed my ribs, tapped against my temples and stretched my fingers. Where else in the world is a half-hour massage thrown in with your haircut? It is completely normal in China, where you can also have a massage while you are out walking in the park. You can even have your hair cut on the pavement in front of your home. Although the end result might not always be what you hoped for, people's goodwill

241

is astounding. In Beijing you can have mineral water delivered to your door just as easily as a train ticket or a PhD from whichever elite university you would like – and it will arrive within an hour. Your fruit seller will peel a pineapple for you on the spot. Try asking a European greengrocer to do that.

Naturally many of these new services exist because of China's inexhaustible reservoir of cheap workers. The army of the urban unemployed alone is estimated to be around 30 million, while in the countryside at least another 200 million are on the look-out for the slightest chance to do something. When your taxi has dropped you off at Beijing's international airport, a group of red-uniformed porters will scrap for the privilege to steer you and your luggage to the check-in for a fee of 10 yuan (less than a pound). All of them were unemployed before, as were the crossing guards in baggy brown uniforms that now terrorize Beijing's cyclists with such curious commands as 'Stop when there's a red light!'. I particularly like to go to the car wash on the Liangma Canal when I have foreign visitors. My friends usually are speechless. Scarcely has the car been driven into the garage and given a quick hosing-down before a swarm of washers descends on it, like a school of piranhas on a cow that has fallen into the Amazonas river. I once counted eight men working at once. You are surrounded by a whirlwind of cloth and chamois. A spray of foam and fountains of water drum on the windows. A staring eye emerges from the spray here, a mop of hair whooshes past there. You barely have time to rub your eyes and the frenzy is already over. Your car is spotless – for 15 yuan.

China is still a developing country, and a foreigner is unimaginably rich to the average Chinese. Should you have a bad conscience when you use such services? I don't think so. The people are nice to you, and you are nice to them and help them to earn their living. The car washers' main work is as security guards at rich people's apartment blocks. They wash cars to earn some extra money on their days off. The handsome hairdresser has just bought himself a car. Nor is it just a question of the money. People in Europe say they want to earn money too. It is a question of people's attitude. Waitresses in China, for example, really are exploited. They often earn little more than 400 yuan a month, plus board and lodging, for working seven days a week – and yet they go about their tasks enthusiastically and happily. If you bring a baby to the restaurant, the waitresses will fight to take the crowing bundle off your hands so that you can enjoy your meal. If you were looking forward to aubergine and there isn't any in the kitchen, then don't be surprised if the chef or a waitress runs off to the market or to a neighbouring restaurant to fulfil your wish. If you are sitting in the 'soft seats' coach of the train, the inspectors will refill your tea cup without being asked. Nor do inspectors or waitresses accept tips. The old Maoist idea that a proud proletarian does not beg has survived remarkably well.

There are exceptions to this rule by now, of course. Hotel porters by now are quite willing to accept the humiliation of a dollar bill. The same goes for the cleaner in the men's toilet in Beijing's live music pub Get Lucky. That was the place where I found out that my old school friend's exclamation did not hold. After two weeks spent among the business-minded

Chinese this friend had exclaimed to me that 'you are only safe from them in the toilet!'. A moment later he stumbled as he tried to escape and was buried immediately under a heap of silk cloth embroidered with peonies and dragons, upon which tumbled piles of pirate DVDs. So he never made it to the toilet. Yet in Get Lucky you are not even safe there. To make the toilet break as interesting as possible, the management has installed flat screens over each urinal. A quick succession of colourful images of the bar's food flickers before your eyes: steak and chips in front of a vase of roses, a hamburger on a blue plastic table-cloth, greasy hot dogs. And while customers are still fumbling to do up their flies, a blossom-white shirt and a bow tie appear at the door to the toilet. 'Yu-hu!' the head that belongs to them shouts, smiling broadly. It is the toilet man. You only realise that he really did mean you when you get to the sink. First, the eager man spreads out a whole row of liquid soaps, lotions and eau de colognes in front of you. Once you start washing your hands he is suddenly behind you, giving you – honest truth – a shoulder and neck massage. Pointless to try to refuse, he wants a tip. From beyond the door Beijing's latest girl punk band are bawling.

Don't forget we are talking about a country that still calls itself 'communist', a country that not long ago was still under the spell of grey-faced, nylon-socks-wearing men and women in state shops whose counters served primarily as a collective resting place for their heads – exhausted from ignoring so many customers. That was the old China, the whole country a cynical commentary on Mao Zedong's battle cry 'serve the people'. People's needs were treated so shabbily that to compensate for that the country invented fairytales with knights in shining armour – and called them model workers. The Beijing bus conductor Li Suli was one of them. The *People's Daily* reported to its amazed readers that she 'was always friendly to the passengers'. (That was enough for her to be raised into the parliament's chairing committee at the next People's Congress.) The Shanghai plumber Xu Hu is also famous. In the 1990s party poets dedicated verses and China's composers wrote hymns to him ('Xu Hu, where are you?'). According to the often-embellished legend the guy's heroic accomplishment was to repair blocked toilets for free in his spare time. Meanwhile, back in dirty reality the Republic was hopping mad because the toilet had flooded again and the only thing the plumber from the work unit who came days later knew to do was to smash the toilet seat. And today? The People's Republic's department stores are open seven days a week, until nine in the evening. Were you to call Chinese Telecom one morning in Beijing and ask for a broadband internet connection, that afternoon the technician would be at your door. Ten minutes later, and only 400 yuan poorer, it's done. Heard that, BT?

But I'll stop there. I can already see all the embassy staffers in Beijing tearing their hair out because civil servants at home might decide to take China off the list of 'hardship postings'. There goes the salary bonus, there go the additional holidays and the sympathy of colleagues too ('Tough chap'). Moreover, China's dark side is not unknown to me. Asking for rice in a restaurant, I too have been answered laconically by the waiters, 'We just ate it up ourselves.' I too have had a cheque returned five times. The first time the employee looked at me as if I was mentally ill and claimed his bank had never accepted cheques; the second time it was returned because my stamp went over the line; the third because we had abbreviated the month of September as '9' rather than the correct '09'; the fourth because against regulations we had used a ball-point pen; and finally because we had used blue rather than black ink.

My suspicion is that this is exactly why we writers like this country so much. Whatever you might say about China at breakfast, by supper-time you can prove the exact opposite to be true (while the breakfast proposition is still holding, of course). No yin without yang. So wait for the chapter in my next book: 'China – service hell'. Until then you can find me in the Cleopatra salon, having my scalp massaged.

共产主义 Gong chan zhu yi

Communism

'Shenme dongxi?' – 'What's that again?'
(recently overheard in the Politburo)

As the country changes, so the language sheds its skin. China's words are marching towards modernity too, and some of the most prominent ones are taking on new meanings, marking the changes along the way. This has to do with politics, because it was not long ago that everything was politics in this country. The powers that be are to blame for the fact that today many words ring hollow and have been worked to death. They are just cracked, dry husks, waiting to disintegrate at the next gust of wind. 'Communism' is one of those words.

Yet society's re-appropriation of concepts can be seen as a sign of its emancipation too. Often the old words are filled with fresh, original meanings – swords are turned into ploughshares. See *tong zhi* (next page).

同志 *Tong zhi*

Comrade Lover

1. Comrade
Once the ubiquitous form of address in China, now as rare as the red Communist or the white Yangtse river dolphin. *Xiao jie* (Miss), *xian sheng* (Mr) and even – Mao help us! – *lao ban* (boss), which were scorned as bourgeois for many years, have come back with a vengeance.

2. Homosexual
The poetic Taiwanese rock star Luo Dayou's song 'Comrade Lover' may have triggered this astounding evolution in meaning. The Hong Kong author and filmmaker Edward Lam then brought the new

251

meaning into common currency shortly afterwards. It soon spread to mainland China. Today China's lesbians and gays call themselves *tong zhi*. There have been no signs of copyright wranglings with the Communist Party as yet. On the contrary, China's homosexuals are enjoying a period of relative tolerance – their collective coming-out in society. Still, at the end of the 1990s when I asked a well-known sexuality researcher in Shanghai for the name of an expert on homosexuality in China, he referred me to a neurologist in Nanjing's Psychiatric Hospital. Then, in 2001, China's Psychiatric Association struck homosexuality off the list of 'perversions' in their handbook on mental illnesses. Today *tong zhi* cover stories sell well in glossy magazines. The literal meaning of *tong zhi* is people who have 'the same goal or concern'.

美 Mei

Beauty
Or: White skin, big eyes

Modern science has taught us that people's perception of beauty is related to the face's symmetry and harmonious proportions. Yet within this framework that our genes have hardwired us, it seems that a society's consensus on what is beautiful is continually negotiable. China has been no different. The well-rounded palace ladies with moon-cake faces that appear on Tang-era figurines only have one thing in common with many skeletal Chinese women today (when anorexia and bulimia are rampant): a preference for pale skin. This is a common symbol of social status in predominantly farming societies, signalling 'I'm not a country woman, I don't need to work in the sun.'

Chinese mothers often say they want their babies to grow up *bai bai pang pang* (white and fat). That may not sound particularly attractive to us, but in China it too is a reminder of a collective memory of tough peasants' lives.

Even common body lotions have bleach added before they reach the shops. When I visited Beijing's Green Links golf club only five out of 250 members were women. This was not due to a lack of emancipation, but rather to their 'fear of the sun'. That at least was the club manager Angela Liu's opinion. She had to battle against her own vanity for more than a year before her love of the sport won out. The five women members have found a solution to their dilemma: they only play at night, under floodlights.

In men this wish to stand apart from the rural workers and the proletariat finds expression in the long nails of their pinkie fingers. On some men it actually has grown into something more like a little trowel. In earlier times overly long fingernails were the privilege of the aristocracy, of anybody who did not need to bundle rice straw or dig out irrigation channels. Noblewomen used to adorn themselves with nail extensions made of silver or gold, giving themselves claws as long as spider's legs. Today a good many taxi drivers and even construction workers have long nails as a display of their social ambitions. Not that they are embarrassed to give them a practical use too, poking them into blocked noses and waxy ears.

No one will be surprised that the Chinese even think of beauty as edible. They have a saying which states exactly that: *xiu se ke can*. In the West we have also heard of the 'almond eyes' and the 'cherry lips' that the writer Cao Xuequin (probably 1715–63) ascribed to one of his heroines. But what about the dainty nose that shone as 'white as soap made from the whitest goose fat'? We might need to see that first. Descriptions by other poets include lovers' cheeks as sweet and smooth 'as a melon ready to be cut', fingers as slim as freshly peeled spring onions and breasts like 'little chicken's heads'.

No aspect of a woman's beauty seemed stranger to Europeans than the 'lotus feet' that for almost a millennium aroused Chinese men, and sometimes sent them into a mad frenzy. They were the 'tender bamboo shoots', the 'white dumplings', the 'pale crescent moons'. Ideally they were curved like eyebrows, small as a mouth and secret as the private parts. Years of torture went into forming them – torture carried out by well-meaning mothers on their four- or five-year-old girls ('You don't want to end up an old spinster!'). China's daughters paid with broken bones, pus, blood and festering flesh, with nights spent screaming and days spent enduring the life of a cripple. All their lives they were never able to go far from their inner chambers (in fact *nei ren* is another word for women: 'those inside'). Barbarism? For a long time the Chinese saw it as the height of civilisation and refinement. After all, this was a custom that was started and brought to perfection in the imperial court. All the tribes and people at the edge of the empire whose women did not bind their feet, they were the barbarians. The lotus lover Fang Xun could not imagine any more intoxicating sight than that of a 'golden lotus', not more than three inches long, held in a man's hand in the flickering light of a lantern.

'Oh! Little feet! You Europeans cannot understand how delicate, how lovely and how exciting it is,' the French doctor J J Matignon, who lived in Beijing was often told. Matignon tried to understand. When foreigners expressed scorn and disgust at the custom, Matignon asked which was more ridiculous: a deformation that makes it difficult for women to walk, or one that displaces the kidneys, squeezes the liver and often makes women infertile? In other words, the European corset.

In some old courtyards in the cities, in the alleys of some remote villages, where girls' feet were bound until the 1940s, you can still find the last women with lotus feet. The day is not far off though when they will take this 1,000-year-old part of China's history into their graves with them. In today's China people find foot binding just as incomprehensible as we find the 19th-century corset. It was Mao's revolutionaries who finally 'liberated the feet' as they called it. Two decades later in the Cultural Revolution (1966–76) these same revolutionaries wanted to eradicate beauty. Wasn't beauty a 'decadent', 'reactionary' concept, like

257

love, music and feudal dances? Wasn't it the expression of a sick individualism that needed to be stamped out for the good of future society? Mao aimed to breed 'new people'. 'The women were sexless, they had sunk even lower than us men,' a contemporary wrote. 'The word "woman" was only used out of habit. They didn't have hips, breasts or behinds.' These words describe the ghostly parade of new arrivals to a labour camp, but actually they also rang true for the rest of the country. The whole of China had become an enormous re-education camp, flirtatious glances had been abolished along with self-respect. 'Don't love make-up and colourful dresses,' the Great Chairman had ordered, 'Love your uniforms!'

The madness has passed, but you can still find people who work at re-educating their compatriots. Anyone trying to find out why China looks like it does, out on the streets and in its offices, will come across Yue-Sai Kan sooner or later. This woman was a TV journalist in America for many years before becoming a missionary for beauty in China. As someone once noted, she is changing China lipstick by lipstick. Kan has had a hand in creating China's new look, especially that of Chinese women. Literally. The eyeshadow of the woman sauntering past you, her bright red lipstick, the elegant arch above her eyes that bends like a weeping willow are probably all courtesy of Yue-Sai. Female readers of Beijing's *Global* magazine voted her 'the most influential Chinese woman of the last 20 years', far ahead of the table tennis legend Deng Yaping. Yue-Sai says that she first brought the world to China and then cultivated the desire for beauty. And the public nods its approval and dips into the rouge-pots from which her striking face greets them. Designers have given this stylised face a timeless, pale quality: you see her bobbed hair, her big eyes and below them her deeply red mouth, like a drop of fire in a snowy land. 'We were the first', these lips whisper. 'Aren't we beautiful?' her coyly sparkling eyes say, 'Aren't we – we Asians?'

小资 *Xiao zi*

Petty bourgeois

Formerly: a dirty word, a thorn in the side of the Revolution, cf. Mao Zedong's 'the tail of the petty bourgeoisie has not been cut off completely yet'. Today: the opposite. With the transition from communism to consumerism the term *xiao zi* in China's cities underwent a remarkable change itself. Not only do young urbanites strive for the life of a 'petty bourgeois', it is even perceived as *ku* (cool) and *lang man* (romantic). Unlike in Great Britain, China's petty bourgeois do not drive Ford Fiestas and put their money into national savings accounts (not yet). The Beijing *xiao zi* drink cappuccino, speak a few words of English, watch the right films (*Amelie*), listen to the right music (Norah Jones), read the right books (Milan Kundera) and frequent the right bar (Suzie Wong). Beijing's metro station kiosks sell a little book that offers tips on how to be a 'young female petty bourgeois'. A test is doing the rounds of the web that lets you know if you are cool middle-class or not. If you are, according to the test, you drink mineral water instead of Coke, you like to sleep naked and you have a rack with at least 30 bottles of red wine in your bedroom. You never wear light-coloured trousers, and you use Anglicisms sparingly but effectively: 'I'm sorry, but I just can't remember how to say that in Chinese.' China's modern petty bourgeoisie is more defined by attitude than by affiliation to an actual class. It is a symptom of a new, pre-packaged individualism as well as of increasing consumerism. Yet the new 'petty bourgeoisie' retains a certain timidity. 'It is not brave,' the Guangzhou newspaper *New Weekly* wrote. In that respect Mao was right, its spirit is hostile to all revolutions. Still, that does not stop it from changing China.

十三亿 *Shi san yi*

1,300,000,000
Rising above the crowd

What does it mean to be one among 1.3 billion people, one of 1,300 million, one of 13,000 lots of 100,000 people? In a country that, although rising, is still poor – where happiness and prosperity seem to be the preserve of only a few? What does it mean to grow up without brothers and sisters because the government has determined – and with some justification – that the country is overcrowded as it is? What does it mean to be a drop in the ocean? To be a footsoldier in that never-ending army of farmers' sons who have left their land to earn a meagre living on construction sites and in foreign companies' factories? To know that these wages will remain among the lowest in the world for decades to come, because there are relatives back home in the villages, hundreds of millions of them, who are only waiting for a vacancy? And what is it like in the cities to rush from school to swimming to piano to English lessons, because you need to outdo the neighbour's child, countless neighbours' children? To squeeze your way onto a chockfull bus every morning so that you can swot away all day in a classroom and all evening under your parents' watchful eyes, so that you are drilled and ready to compete for one of the few places at a school that will prepare you for the college entrance exam, a college that will help you to snatch one of the rare places at a good university, which again is the only option that promises a career and good money? For that is what people here call the good life – being one of the handful of people who have access to this gold dust.

Tai jiao, 'foetal education', is now common practice in China. Unborn babies are played recordings of Tang poems and Mozart's string quartets in order to give them a better starting position for the rat race. After all, every little Chinese baby shares his birthday with 25,000 others, a competitor every one of them. A friend of mine bought CDs that had been produced just for this purpose – by the 'Nanjing Unborn Babies' University'.

Tang Xiaoyan is a Shanghainese who went to study in New Zealand. Two months after arriving there she wrote a letter to a Shanghai newspaper. She asked why so many Chinese students at her university had so few Kiwi friends. It was their own fault, she argued. 'They study as hard as they can and don't have time to do anything else.' For her fellow Chinese being a student was just part of their struggle to survive. 'The strong sense of competition and real pressure means that young Chinese people are very pragmatic. They often sacrifice their happiness for what they call a better life.' As Tang noticed, Shanghai girls mainly want three things of a prospective husband: he must have money, his own house and a car. 'That has completely altered the meaning of love, but the girls know that without money, a house and a car their lives will be tough.'

If you walk into a bookshop in China, you will soon

find that the most prominent displays are not stacks of contemporary fiction, but mountains of garishly advertised self-help titles often translated from English, such as *How I Succeeded at Harvard University*, *Becoming a Millionaire in Minutes* and *China's Jews: The Business Strategies of Wenzhou's Entrepreneurs*. The precarious state of the Chinese publishing industry is a major factor here. Such books both sell well and are politically unproblematic. But it also reflects the ruthless competition. 'The percentage of people here who want to get on in life is much higher than in well-established societies like America,' says Peggy Yu, the managing director of Dangdang.com, China's largest online bookstore.

To succeed in life some people learn a profession, others study the ways of the Party. Hao Lulu made herself beautiful. The process lasted half a year, but the 24-year-old feels like a new person now. In high spirits she tells me that she's bagged three already, honestly! Was she cutting notches in her lipstick case by now? No, she replies with a coquettish smile. Bored as she was, she had just been sitting in the passenger seat and let her gaze sweep over Beijing's roaring traffic (her artfully posed eyes gazing from under lids that now have a new, a Western fold). Then her gaze caught his in a passing car. She only held his gaze, nothing else, Hao Lulu insists. Held it for a tiny little while only. Until the bang of a car crash interrupted them. Three men in three days had preferred to gamble with their cars rather than stop looking at this woman. Each time as she drove off, she could not help having a good laugh, she says. 'I'm a bad girl, aren't I?' She purses her lips, her real ones, into a pout, and then laughs. 'The best thing about it was that the cars were a Lexus and two Mercedes', she confides. Nothing but the best. All in all, Hao Lulu says, she feels fantastic.

Her lips weren't altered, they are a present from her parents, as are her teeth, her chin and her hands. The rest of this vision sitting before us though is as much a work of art as of nature. Its creation required a cabinet of scalpels and one young woman, Hao Lulu, a Beijinger of humble background. Her father is a football coach, her mother a bookkeeper. She learnt the jewellery trade – and how to give men the eye.

'Beautiful girls have more opportunities,' she says. It is as simple as that. 'Women should know what they want,' she adds. Hao Lulu did not undergo plastic surgery because she wanted to buy herself self-confidence, but because she already had it. She is quite open about it. She wants something in life and she knows how to get it. No wonder Hao Lulu has become a media celebrity, she fits this place at this time.

Hao Lulu was never ugly. The worst you could say about her was that she looked 'average'. But she had been dreaming of a new nose, at least, since she was 16. And the plastic surgery clinic that had opened only a year before was in urgent need of something to give its sluggish trade a boost. Bao Huai, the marketing manager of the Beijing Evercare Clinic had a brainwave. Why not find a nice girl, do her up from top to toe, and then reap the headlines? He mentioned it to his friend Hao Lulu and she was excited about the idea too. Her lively personality was perfect for the television teams that lapped up the story: for the first time in China there was a complete overhaul of a person.

How often then did the surgeons work on her during those six months? After all, her eyes, nose, neck, breasts, waist, bottom, hips and thighs are all new. 'A good dozen times,' says the happy recipient. Television cameras followed it all. Evercare's turnover increased so much at each new operation that its director Li Jing rushes over to Hao Lulu when she enters the clinic, greeting her with shrill exclamations: 'My precious girl! My boss!' Evercare now owns three clinics in Beijing, with 120 employees and a turnover of three million yuan every month. 'From next year we hope to raise that to 40 to 50 million yuan,' the director Li tells me. Seriously, a 15-fold increase? 'Only drug trafficking would be more lucrative right now,' says Bao Huai earnestly, himself rather intoxicated.

Young women's lives have, here too, been taken over by the need to look chic. Many would agree with Hao Lulu when she says 'I dream of a life as a *xiao zi*, a petty bourgeois – drinking tea with friends, going to the gym, shopping, certainly not worrying about money or working hard.' Hao Lulu is admired for her burning desire for a life of middle-class hedonistic ease. For most women in this country that means one thing: finding the right man. 'Let's not fool ourselves,' she says. 'This society is still dominated by men.'

That is true. And terribly unjust all the same when you look at Chinese women. They are strong women who start up companies, run laboratories and drive stubborn water buffalo through rice fields. At the time of writing this book only one of China's 100 largest companies has a woman as its CEO: the Baoshan steelworks in Shanghai. In some places things are getting worse. The Communist Party's Central Committee only has five women in it, compared to 193 male members. The number was never as low as it is now. Even the mass redundancies of the crumbling state companies affect women more than men. Perhaps the statistic that gives most pause for thought is this one: China is the only country in the world where more women commit suicide than men. Most are rural women who take poison.

One of the only promising strategies for upward mobility is to hook an alpha male. And Evercare's helpers are there to create the bait. 'Since Hao Lulu, the demand for full-body makeovers has skyrocketed,' reports director Li. Four of every ten customers are single, often discouraged, women. 'A woman's beauty is her capital, that's how it is here.' What is the prize that you can buy with it? 'It's got to be a man with a house and a car,' the journalist and scriptwriter Meng Danfeng told me. 'As a girl in China your only chance is a wealthy man. If you don't get one, then you'll still be slogging away as a worker in a factory or as a farmhand when you are forty,' a painter friend of mine said. She herself has never even worn make-up. 'Some parents only eat steamed bread rolls, starving themselves to save up for their daughter's operation. I can understand that.'

二奶 *Er nai*

Mistress

An accessory, like a man's black leather handbag and the Audi coupé with tinted windows. As the new elite imitates the old mandarins more and more, it was only a matter of time before the revival of the age-old practice of keeping concubines. Among the rich and powerful it is now good form to have an *er nai* (literally: second wife), and to pay for her own apartment, little car, and a great many handbags. Which the mistress then insists the man carry for her as a signal to other women that he is taken. We're not talking about love, we're talking about a deal: sex and an ego-boost in exchange for upkeep. China's National Women's Association at one point

271

demanded that unfaithful men be sent to labour camps, but its campaign did not get far: 'Because the men in this country who keep mistresses are the same ones who make the laws,' as one online commentator complained. The government at least pretends to be worried. 'Bigamy and the keeping of concubines undermine our social fabric,' the news agency New China protested, 'and the involvement of civil servants is a blot on our government's image.' Guangzhou authorities took to court the mistress of the former deputy police minister Li Jizhou, who is in prison for corruption. She was accused of participating in the smuggling of 262 luxury cars. More bad news for the 'second wives' comes from their stronghold in southern China. Hong Kong men unhappy in their marriages cross the border into southern China in their tens of thousands, looking for happiness or at least good meals from rural women from Sichuan and Anhui. Whole 'mistress villages' were established. And now? Hong Kong has passed its zenith. Hong Kongers are being made redundant by their companies, and their mistresses by them.

自由 *Zi you*

Freedom
The March of Privacy

China: a land of freedom. Yes, the same land where a 22-year-old student can disappear into prison for a year without an arrest warrant or court proceedings for no other reason than that she was guilty of a fine sense of irony. (She suggested on the internet that everyone in China should stop lying for 24 hours, or better yet, should go out onto the streets and preach Marx and Lenin to the people, to test their popularity.) But in some ways you could say that people here are even freer than elsewhere. 'You can sing at the top of your voice as you're cycling along or scrubbing yourself down in the public bath house – and no one will bat an eyelid,' a Beijing friend said to me. 'You can wander around in the streets in your pyjamas all day, walk backwards through the city and hug trees in the park – and you'll just be one of many doing the same thing. Those things are all considered normal in China. Plus you can eat anything that crawls the earth.' You can also flatten pig's heads with a steamroller and put them under glass, sew living crabs together into a moving curtain and surgically connect mice at the ribs before putting them into a goldfish bowl, and by doing so make a name for yourself as an avant-garde artist. If European curators still don't come knocking, you can head to a hospital's pathology department where you will always find staff who are willing to sell you a fresh corpse. If you buy dead babies, you then can make them part of an installation and let your freshly drawn blood dribble into their lifeless mouths, as we experienced one Easter Saturday in Beijing's Sculpture Institute. You can also cut off part of the dead baby's flesh and take a bite. The artist Zhu Yu did just that in his aptly named 'Cannibal' performance in Shanghai. As he explained afterwards, he created his work 'in the gap between morality and law.'

China has developed an active young art scene whose artists nowadays preferably band together in gutted factories. The colours and forms they experiment with are of a quality so individualistic and counterrevolutionary that it makes one wonder why the embalmed Mao has not long chosen to resurrect himself and enact a Final Judgment. China's avant-garde has even begun to creep into its own country's public awareness, rather than just to produce art for European and American collectors. This itself is a minor sensation. Nor would I wish to imply that all the artists dedicate themselves to shocking for shock's sake. It is certainly true though that in this country, where until recently artists had to 'be one with the emotions and thoughts of the masses' (Mao Zedong), today things happen that would be immediately banned in the West. Not that they are expressly allowed in China, it is just that no one cares about them any more. Maybe by now the police have also noticed that most young artists anyway are more interested in fame and fortune than in rebellion. The much rumoured 'underground' has been turned into a profitable means to this end. Nowadays it's more often a marketing ploy than a symptom of real repression: foreigners love the frisson of what is forbidden, and the customer is now king in this country too … The matter of artistic freedom is a complex one in China. Chinese have only known the term *zi you*, freedom, since the mid-19th century. It was imported via Japan, along with its cousins 'democracy' (*min zhu*) and 'human rights' (*ren quan*). To this day this bunch of immigrants still seems rather suspect to some Chinese, in particular those in power and those of a Confucian persuasion. Freedom to them has a whiff of the irresponsible and anti-social about it – threatening, in any case. Yet eternal China is constantly changing. 'A silk dipped in a blue dye will turn blue, dipped in yellow dye it will turn yellow,' as the philosopher Mozi (486–376 BC) once said. 'That is not only true of silk, but also of a person or a country… A country can change through the influences to which it is exposed.'

A pre-condition of freedom is the individual. *Zi you*'s literal meaning is 'following yourself', 'starting from yourself'. Which is only one more reason why the word has a bad reputation. Almost exactly 100 years ago a Chinese wrote the following: 'Although the concept of the "individual" was only introduced to China three or four years ago, people who claim to understand our times see it as an unbearable stigma. Someone who is called an individualist is immediately considered guilty of high treason.'

While today a young Chinese pop star sings 'Live out your I/every day / you always have your unchanging, wonderful I, oh, I / you want freedom / don't be afraid of what others say / just be yourself.' This song by the Hong Kong singer Kelly is called 'Shine Every Day'. I saw it being performed in a television broadcast from an open air music festival in the city of Kunming. The fact that you could see her lip-synch this hymn to individuality in front of an audience that had been given identical T-shirts and red baseball caps by the organisers, and where everybody waved little Chinese flags back and forth to the same beat, made the scene even more fitting a picture for China's colliding worlds.

I met Hao Feng in Beijing's Haidian, the university district. A former philosophy and political science student, Hao wrote a book in 1996 about the American grunge rock band Nirvana and its singer Kurt Cobain – and promptly opened a bookshop to sell it: symptomatic of the Chinese enterprising spirit. His shop stocked the works of Albert Camus and poetry by Jack Kerouac and Arthur Rimbaud – it basically was a loss-making venture that he financed from the amazingly good sales of his Nirvana book. 'China is still very hierarchical, the state still has its fingers in too many pies. Things can only get better,' Hao Feng says. 'But what a dog's fart, this "modernisation" that our leaders promise. It can't work until people find themselves. How else can they be creative? In my books I show young people that there are alternatives to school, university, graduation, job. Individualism used to be a rude word here. I say it's progress.' Rock stars and poets who die young from drug excesses exert as much of a fascination on Hao Feng as they do on Westerners of his generation. At the time we met he was writing a biography of Jim

Morrison and The Doors. Hao Feng also works for MTV's Chinese subsidiary. 'I'm optimistic. Society is separating itself from politics, people's attitudes are getting healthier,' he says. 'People are creating their own spaces that have nothing to do with the Party: they go to university, earn money, write books, go to gay bars. None of that is a problem any more, in spite of the Party's fear of pluralism and of books. How stupid of them – when people have ways to let off steam, when there are ways out and niches, then nothing's going to explode.'

Things are a colourful mix in today's China. Few people still like reading poems or reflecting about society or politics, the Party has successfully eradicated all that, but young people especially redecorate the spaces of their private lives every day. They no longer let politicians tell them what to do, instead they listen to the same trendsetters that determine how their contemporaries in Taiwan and Hong Kong furnish their lives. The prepackaged, consumption-driven ideas of individuality that we already know in the West are conquering China – only they are pursued with far fewer inhibitions in East Asia. It's Starbucks and Ikea for the upwardly mobile female office workers, chic Korean clothes for the teenagers. China's urban youth has a ravenous hunger for trends from richer, more developed foreign countries. Its own television programmes are still too grey and schoolmasterly, its actors too full of pathos and its singers too stiff. Against which the television series from Korea are fresh and cool, and their Asian faces and shared customs make them more familiar than the Hollywood imports. As one female student enthused, 'the girls are so beautiful and the boys are all a dream.' Korea's manufactured stars won't have anything to do with sex and drugs – that too goes down well in China.

Conservative Chinese are still shocked though, that the direction of cultural exchange could be reversed, and that the young heirs of their 5,000-year-old culture could succumb to 'cultural kimchi', as one commentator called it. He was alluding to Korea's national dish of spicy pickled cabbage: 'unappetizing food without any nutritional value', as he saw it. One commentator noted rightly that many of the cultural phenomena from Korea are in fact re-imports from the West, be it blond hair, nose rings or the baggy hip hop trousers. He thus supposed that *'nouveau riche Korea'* had an 'inferiority complex' towards the West, and that China in consequence has a 'double inferiority complex'. While in fact his grumpy polemic only goes to show a decisive reason for the longing look of young people beyond their country's borders: China's double pleasure deficit.

Yet hedonism has made headway in the youth culture. Nothing shows that more clearly than young people's attitude towards sex. When the poet Yang Lian visited Beijing from his London exile, he was amazed. 'Sexual revolution? No time for revolution here, they're too busy having sex.' Yesterday the state ordained prudishness, and suddenly: anything goes. Not long ago a premarital or extramarital affair could land you in a labour camp. When the police recently caught hotel guests in a threesome in Shenyang they let them go again because the prosecutor couldn't decide whether their act still constituted an indecency in this Republic or whether it was a private matter among the three of them. The new sexual freedom goes hand in hand with the discovery of privacy. The Chinese have long had a character for 'private': *si*. Yet the level of esteem with which private matters were held in China can been seen in the fact that *si* means not only 'private' but also 'egoistical'. So far almost all words that include *si* have negative connotations – be it 'self-seeking', 'smuggling' or 'nepotism'. Mao's total-itarianism only intensified Chinese culture's disdain for privacy and erased any separation between private and public spaces. The last little coil in your brain had to bend to the will of the Great Chairman. The new appreciation of the private is a sign that Chinese society is shrugging off the memory of that era. It is no coincidence that it comes simultaneously with the Communists' rehabilitation of private industry. (The Party even wrote new protections for private industry into the constitution.) Marx was right: it is the social being of people that determines their consciousness

香体珠 *Xiang ti zhu*

Deodorant

One of the few things hard to come by in China (cf. Bakewell tart and formerly also Nutella). The lack of this toiletry that was as instrumental in the civilisation of the West as the printing press and the separation of powers, illustrates one more exception to the rule that all people are equal. Maybe they are in God's eyes, but not in front of his nose. Europeans smell, the Chinese don't. Or rather, when they do, it is only the garlic on their breath, but never their armpits that stink. One Beijing city magazine recommended two solutions to foreigners: (1). The surgical removal of their sweat glands, available from local hospitals for £100, done in an hour. (2). A pharmaceutical spray by the lovely name of *hu xiu sha jun*, literally: bacteria killer for people who stink like foxes. For us foreigners, in other words. Deodorant sales are picking up in major cities, though the sticks are used not to prevent sweat and bad smells but instead more like perfume. Hence its name: *xiang ti zhu* means 'pearls for a sweet-smelling body'.

成语 *Cheng yu*

Proverbs

Wisdom, normally condensed to four characters. This people's experience in its most concentrated form. For example, 'the chancellor's stomach is spacious enough for ships to navigate'. (I wouldn't even want to know what that means, you can spin all manner of yarns around it.) *Cheng yu* often allude to philosophy, literature and historical anecdotes, and serve as proof of their speaker's education. They have multiplied over the centuries and are capable of fatally wounding the pride and self-confidence of any learner of Chinese. After years of study, most students of Chinese reach the point where they come to believe that they have a reasonable grasp of the language, and are enjoying people's flattery at parties (Foreigner: 'Hi.' Chinese: 'Oh, your Chinese is excellent!'). You might start to prattle away happily, basking in your eloquence. You chat, joke, laugh and cross swords over the revaluation of the renminbi currency (well, actually over football), until your conversation partner suddenly says, 'Tiger's head, snake's tail'. Sorry? 'It's obvious,' your Chinese acquaintance continues, 'push three, stop four'. There is only one thing that is obvious to you – he most probably is not talking football tactics. So you grin sheepishly, nod an 'of course!' and quickly run off 'for a drink'. Some of the sayings explain themselves: 'When you enter a village, follow its customs.' Unfortunately those are in the minority. In my case at least, my Chinese acquaintances generally 'play the zither for the cow' (cast their pearls before swine), when they exclaim 'Sai weng shi ma' (the old man at the border has lost his horse). It would only have made sense to me had I known that the horse later returns to the old man, accompanied by a second horse. A stroke of luck, then? That furthermore the old man then gave his son the second horse and the son was promptly thrown and broke his leg. So, a case of bad luck? That finally the broken leg prevented the son from being recruited into the army. Ah, a heaven-sent gift! So these four characters hide an entire story: never rush to conclusions about whether something is for better or worse, the world always has another surprise waiting.

The world? China.

小贴士

Final tips

When you return to Beijing

Don't be surprised if the 'Beijing feeling' starts to creep up your spine. Once a European composer returned to the city he knew from his days as a student. 'It's crazy,' he stammered, after he found his voice again. 'You come back just two years later – and Beijing no longer exists. Gone, vanished. Instead there is a new city, and it is also called Beijing.'

The city does not merely shed its skin, it's about to remove its very core. Visitors like to call it dynamism, but for many inhabitants it is a cross they bear: they cannot keep pace with their own city. Foreigners least of all. In the West you call a restaurant to reserve a table for that evening, in Beijing you call up first too – to make sure the restaurant still exists. Perhaps you think I am joking. So do our friends, until they visit us in Beijing. One couple stayed with us for a month. On Christmas Eve we set off for a feast in the famous Hot Pot King restaurant. At first we thought we must have got its address wrong. We hadn't. But on the spot where the restaurant should have been we were greeted by a giant construction pit. We went to the Golden Mountain Village instead, where the food is just as delicious – two weeks later it was demolished as well. As was our favourite Japanese restaurant soon afterwards. It has been going on like this for years. I have given up counting how many times I stood in front of gaping pits. I just fondly remember some of my favourite places that are now gone for good: a cosy noodle bar here, an old theatre there – in exchange for which the city now has Asia's largest office and shopping block (a building that in the ideal world of my dreams would be reason enough to take urban planners and architects to court). Yes, that Beijing feeling. It is an offshoot of the Beijing rule that bad-tempered gods have cursed the city with. The rule goes like this: '(1). Nothing lasts. (2). Certainly not beautiful and homely things.' There is no need to cultivate the Beijing feeling, it ambushes you every time you find a new little wonder: a courtyard house from a century long past, an enchanting lakeside bar. These are little oases that leave you speechless. Out of joy? Only partly. Something creeps up your spine, floods your chest and takes your heart in its pincer grip – fear. Fear, worry and sorrow, as if you were looking at a dead man walking. This once imperial city is erasing itself to prepare for reincarnation: as a profitable, modern, ugly, planless city.

But wait, there is news of a plan. The city government called together 200 academics and 70 research institutes to swap ideas. A high-ranking member of the city's planning commission presented the results to the public in 2005. As *China Daily* wrote: 'The revised plan introduces the concept of "building a society suitable for living" as the city's development target for the first time.' In case you missed that: building a society suitable for living. For the first time – 800 years after the city was founded, 56 years after the People's Republic was established. That is the kind of city this is, that is the kind of people who run it.

I called it the Beijing feeling, but actually it can overwhelm you wherever you are in China. How did it come to this intoxication with speed, this orgy of change for change's sake? Did it need a country that had stagnated and trodden water as long as this one had? A hundred years ago people complained that you could not move a table in China without blood being shed. China today: there is no lack of profit or excitement, just sometimes of clear thinking, and always of soul.

Secret tip 1

> Close your eyes, and you will soon feel
> at home in Beijing again. No, you won't
> recognise it with your nose either – not
> since the last of the Uighur kebab sellers
> were driven off the streets. But your ears
> … just prick up your ears, can you hear it

now? Your taxi driver, who soundtracks
the journey from the airport to your hotel
with a monologue of curses; the ebb and
swell of cicadas chirping in the trees when
you get out of the taxi; the celestial wailing
of a turning flock of pigeons equipped
with little whistles on their legs by their
breeders; the cheerful chaos that rings out
from the neighbouring restaurant. And
finally, in your room: that glugging of the
hot water pipes, as if the building has got
wind, that you nearly forgot; that familiar
hammering from next door and the dearly
loved scream of a drill from the floor below.
Ah, back in Beijing.

And now: bury your head under your
pillow.

How to cross a street in China

China's drivers don't learn to drive on city streets,
but on specially-created training grounds outside the
cities. Anything else would be too dangerous – for the

driving instructors. Their safety is of utmost importance as they will supply the fresh crop of drivers to replace all those former learners who usually waste no time in forcing each other off the roads. To judge by appearances, the driving schools work with the latest teaching materials from Rome and Mogadishu, while taking into account 'Chinese characteristics'. (The fact, for example, that the lights on buses and other large vehicles over 7.5 tonnes are to be turned off punctually at nightfall.) The following manoeuvres are taught: taking the right-hand lane to turn left; taking the left-hand lane to turn right; staying in the middle, and still turning off. Then there is simple overtaking on the curb side, as well as overtaking while cutting into the cycle lane; which again is followed by 'advanced curb-side overtaking'. That allows you to mow down not more than two cyclists on a sunny day (the exception for rainy days can be viewed in the relevant government departments). As an accommodation to the Chinese love of flocking together you are finally taught freestyle-crossing at central traffic nodes. This requires firstly all the cars to end up as entangled as possible, and secondly the disregard of all rules of logic and self-interest. Creating a traffic jam in Beijing long after midnight will bring bonus points and a honourable mention in the newspapers' sports pages. This is a popular exercise for advanced learners and normally all that it calls for are two vehicles moving towards each other at an empty crossroads. They then form the core for the docking manoeuvres of the other cars.

Learners must also pass a written driving test. Around 110,000 people a year die on China's roads, according to Guangzhou's Jinan University. That is world record, both in absolute terms and in relation to the number of cars. It comes as no surprise then that in the Chinese film, *The Test Family*, a driving examiner asks the candidates: 'Suddenly you see a pedestrian and a dog in front of you – which one do you run over: the person or the dog?' (The right answer being: 'Neither, you brake.') Army and embassy staff are exempt from driving school.

Traffic in Chinese cities is living (well, mostly living) Darwinism. Down at the bottom you can find the grey-haired backwards-walkers creeping through the jungle of streets: easy prey. Then come the average forwards-walkers. They form an amazingly robust species that does not let traffic lights, fences or approaching cars divert it from its migratory behaviour; it holds its ground through the strength of its numbers. A little higher in the chain come the few remaining cyclists, who once in Beijing's distant past inhabited the savannahs of the city; then come the tricycle riders that frustrated policemen enjoy chasing because they cannot turn easily and generally offer their throats submissively to hunters. Above them on the evolutionary scale comes (a) the car-driving young bloods; (b) the mandarins hovering behind their Mercedes' tinted windows; and (c) the lorry drivers, who fly somewhere beyond good and evil. ('It's still smoking' is a good enough reason in China for a lorry to be considered roadworthy.) The above-mentioned military and embassy drivers are right at the top of the pyramid, without any natural competitors. They are allowed to overtake on pavements and to bag a maximum of three traffic policemen per day.

For everyone else driving a car in China is not unlike a video game. Our tradition of concentrating on the road in front of you is taboo in China. Instead you must use 180-degree vision, keeping track simultaneously of every moving object and all the gaps between them, as if you were watching a radar screen. This enables you to slalom instinctively through the flood of metal. Thankfully traffic in Beijing flows sluggishly, sometimes excessively so. *China Daily* recently reported a traffic jam in north Beijing that the police took 'two nights and three days' to remove.

Secret tip 2

For pedestrians: always look both ways
before you cross the street.

For drivers: if you return to your
homeland after many years' driving
in China, for God's sake don't sit in
a car. Contact your probation officer
immediately, he will guide you through
the rehabilitation programme to which you
are entitled.

Where English is spoken

Congratulations to all of you who were planning to use drugs or visit prostitutes in China. Wise move to wait until after 2004, that being the year when the Chinese police, at least on paper, renounced the use of torture. Or rather, it is no longer worthwhile to torture suspects because the courts officially no longer recognise confessions extracted under torture. However, according to the new rules this, only applies to minor 'administrative crimes' like those mentioned above. Burglars, saboteurs, followers of religions whose practice includes certain gymnastic exercises and other hardened criminals are advised to go and find themselves a different field of operations.

More good news: foreigners in police custody now have the right to an interpreter. The police in the capital are even busy learning English themselves. After all, the 2008 Olympic Games with all the exciting possibilities for intercultural interrogation are just around the corner. In Beijing's bookshops you can buy the 'Olympic Security English' textbook that is preparing China's police force for every eventuality. In the very first chapter an observant constable comes across a rather clueless foreign reporter who, in answer to the question of what he is doing, replies in all honesty that he is working on a story about the outlawed Falun Gong sect. 'But Falun Gong has nothing to do with the Games,' the policeman instructs him. 'It's beyond the limit of your coverage and illegal,' and promptly escorts the journalist to the police station, 'to clear up this matter'. Cooperative foreigners would also do well to learn the book's dialogues. In the conversation 'We stop a stolen car' on page 121 a British woman called Helen is dragged out of the car and off to a police station. 'You're violating my human rights!' she protests. 'What lousy luck!' The trained constable's correct answer: 'No tricks! Don't move!'

Once you really immerse yourself in the roleplays, you will soon realise that the polyglot policewomen can be both vigilant and empathetic. One policewoman, for example, confronts an Afghan who has broken into an American's hotel room. The Afghan wants to take his revenge for the bombing of his homeland, where his family lost their lives. 'We feel sympathy for your misfortune,' she comforts him, before continuing in a tougher vein to say that this is still no reason to harass innocent Americans, 'especially during the Olympic Games'.

The guardians of law and order can also make foreigners happy. They return the wallet that a tourist had left in a taxi. 'It's really incredible!' exclaims tourist Joe Kennedy on page 55. 'A lost wallet can be recovered! Only in Beijing can this be possible!'

Secret tip 3

> Be prepared for everything when you come
> to Beijing. It really is incredible, the things
> that can only happen here.

If you are planning a trip

Fetch your diary and make a note of three dates: the Spring Festival (in January or February, the exact date changes according to the moon calendar), Labour Day (1 May), and the National Holiday (1 October). Then take a red pen and write in big letters besides those dates: STAY HOME! Because that is when the

Chinese travel. All of them at once – well, almost. The Chinese Ministry of Railways was proud to announce that it had carried over 149 million passengers last Spring Festival. They will all be sitting in your carriage. At least, that is how it will seem to you if you ignore this warning.

Travel is a relatively new development. For 50 years the Chinese working class did what it did best: it worked and worked, and then it worked some more. Sometimes for a change the workers would cheer on their great leaders. The word 'vacations' did not exist. Then in 1999, exactly half a century after Mao liberated China, a new revolution arrived. China was given holidays: a week off at each of the three dates listed above. Since then even the urban proletariat has been gripped by the travel bug. Former textile factory workers, cooks and taxi drivers do something completely new: they travel. They march into travel shops, ask for as long a flight as possible, and find themselves airborne for the first time in their lives, begging their neighbour for the window seat on their way to Yunnan, where China borders the

Golden Triangle. At least, that is what my wonderful cleaning lady did in 2002, for the first time in all her 65 years. On arrival Mrs Yang and her husband were treated to colourful spectacles by minority peoples, as well as fried scorpions and pickled tree bark for supper, a risqué dance show by Thai transsexuals, overpriced tat in the shops and great opportunities to pose in front of elephants and pagodas of all sizes. A real package holiday, in other words. 'Flying was the best bit,' she told me happily afterwards, giggling as she showed us her souvenir: a DVD of the transsexuals' show. She wants to go on a trip again soon.

Going on holiday is even a patriotic act now. Every yuan that Mrs Yang spends is a service to her country. China's rulers want its people to bring their savings into circulation in uninhibited holiday spending on trains, hotels, Polaroid photos, laughing Buddhas carved out of jade, silk carpets and talking stamp albums ('Hold high the banner of Deng Xiaoping Theory'). The planners have even invented a phrase for this: the holiday economy. It is a wonderful thing. If you like to row oar-to-oar on the misty West Lake, be pushed off the Great Wall, asphyxiated in the Forbidden City and not be able to catch a glimpse of the sea for the mass of black rubber tyres in which summer holidaymakers are merrily rocking tummy-to-tummy ('cooking dumplings' is the Chinese expression for this). Nor can you have such a holiday without a fight for the best, the only spot for that most important event: the solemn pose for the camera.

Secret tip 4

How can I mingle with a Chinese tour group and not attract attention?

Pack a week's rations of melon pips, fruit, beef jerky and eggs pickled in tea and, above all, all your living relatives into a bus. If you are going off for more than an afternoon, double the rations.

Then take pictures of every rock, tree and foreigner that crosses your path. Don't take any of these photos without placing yourself or your mother/daughter/aunt/ grandmother in the picture – better yet, they can all take turns to be in the picture. No matter how deep the drop is from the rocky ledge you are balancing on, stand as straight as a People's Army soldier as you stare into the camera, thumbs on trouser seams (alternatively, young women may hold their fingers out in a cheeky V for Victory). While other foreigners are still taking pictures of the old pagoda on the mountain, turn to the actual photogenic scene: the giant VW Polo billboard on the other side.

Ask at least every two hours for hot water to pour on the tea leaves in your jam jar.

Climbing one of the sacred 10,000-foot peaks or a dilapidated part of the Great Wall, make sure if you are a woman that you wear at least three-inch heels, and if you are a man that you roll your trousers up over your knees and your shirt up to your armpits so that you can beat out a

rhythm on your stomach during picnic
breaks.

Always follow the guide's megaphone.
It can generally still be heard over half a
mile away, piping out 'My heart will go
on'. Be careful to not follow any of the
other 12 megaphones blaring 'My heart
will go on'.

Don't be surprised if you are greeted in the lobby of
a top hotel by a two-layered Glockenspiel, where traditional European figures circle around the top layer
as they do on the Swiss Centre's famous Glockenspiel
in Leicester Square, while on the second layer Walt
Disney's Seven Dwarves dance around Snow White.
Under the Glockenspiel you could well also see a giant
fresco based on Leonardo da Vinci's 'Last Supper'.
You might find that the copyist, having obviously
found the original too boring, has added a whole
circus of dwarves, jugglers and half-naked women,
one of whom holds out her hand to the man with
the halo. Don't be surprised either if the waitress in

the hotel café informs you that the picture represents 'the marriage of Jesus and Mary'. That is just what happened to me in Qingdao.

Perhaps only Americans love kitsch as much as the Chinese, whether in the arts or in music. It probably was music of the deceptively named 'easy listening' kind that the late reformer Deng Xiaoping had in mind when he started his programme of reforms in the early 1980s and said with a shrug, 'When you open a window, some flies will come in.' Although if he had foreseen the consequences of China's new openness, he might have reconsidered. 'Easy listening' is a jumble of notes originally employed in Europe and North America for the good purpose of inducing mild delirium in patients undergoing root canal surgery. It was only when it reached China that it got completely out of control, penetrating every last Manchu's hammer, anvil and stirrup bones. In one particularly severe case in the mid-1980s, Richard Clayderman's 'Ballade pour Adeline', found itself chased out of Europe, slipped past the border guards and evaded quarantine. Since then it has made its permanent home in the Harbin church tower's loudspeaker and in several fountains in Guangzhou, from where it will torture passers-by until the end of time. Everywhere in China the old propaganda cassettes have been replaced by light music on an endless loop, for example on 18-hour train journeys where the constant music clanging out of cheap audio equipment has the same effect on passengers as the old tapes did: under the pretence of inducing moments of happiness they render independent thinking impossible.

Secret tip 5

> Leave at home your underwear, travel
> guide, wristwatch, diarrhoea tablets, credit
> card and dictionary and you can still have a
> great trip, but one thing you should never
> ever forget: ear plugs.

By now you can see a punk sporting a green mohawk advertising China Telecom on television. Ronald McDonald has arrived in China too. He is called

Mai Danglao Shushu, Uncle McDonald. Yet for any nostalgic visitors, here are a few reminders that China is still a socialist state:

- There is no first class rail travel, instead there is 'soft sleep' and 'hard sleep', 'soft seat' and 'hard seat'.
- There are still restaurants where yawning waiters pull the artificial turf out from under your feet at eight on the dot – beware: state owned enterprise!
- The hand towels in a good many hotels are made of some guaranteed water-repellent material. (Most probably a spin-off of Chinese space research.)
- Hotel televisions do not have porn channels.

And yet you also notice that China is not a socialist state any more when the phone in your hotel room rings. While still half asleep you hear vaguely familiar words purring sweetly into your ear, sounding vaguely like *'Tshiipa, tshiipa'*, *'Baby'* and *'Ma-shaji'*. *Ma-sha-ji* literally means 'horse kills cock', but here it would primarily refer to the less bloody activity defined by the similar-sounding English word 'massage'. The word stands for a whole raft of services that the *xiao jie*, the lady on the other end of the line, is ready to negotiate on a one-to-one basis. Businesses offering a similar range of services are often disguised as hairdressers. You really do just want a haircut and a strictly medical shoulder and neck massage? Then you would do best to avoid all those hairdressers' shops where you see a dozen slim legs in hot pants gyrating in the doorway, while a chorus of young hairdressers trills a cheerful 'Yu-hu!' – apparently aimed at you.

Secret tip 6

Those of us living in Beijing occasionally come down with fits of nostalgia for the planned economy. Then all we do to get our taste of the old days again is step into any of the city's banks and drive its employees and ourselves crazy with such exotic requests as 'a money transfer',

'cashing a cheque' or 'paying a telephone
bill'. Scary stuff. Try it.

Some visitors complain bitterly about how this taxi
driver in Xi'an, or that dumpling seller in Hangzhou
ripped them off. They come to the sad conclusion that in this country swindling foreigners is a
national sport. Actually, it is. There is a wonderful
essay titled 'To screw foreigners is patriotic', written
by the Australian sinologist Geremie Barmé. I know
what he means by that. Once, after a five-minute
ride, a Beijing rickshaw driver demanded double
the agreed price, using the old trick, 'The price we
agreed on was for only one of you, not both.' The
man followed us into a restaurant and made a scene.
He even had the balls to clutch at his heart and
theatrically exclaim, 'You foreigners! You've been
duping us Chinese for 150 years!' If I had not already
been immensely hungry and annoyed by that time,
I would have laughed out loud. And it would not
have surprised me if the rickshaw driver had done
the same. For many mainland stall-holders, cooks

and rickshaw drivers conning rich people is indeed a sport. (Every Westerner is rich in the eyes of most Chinese.) And you make life much easier for yourself if you see it in a similarly playful, sporting way. You will travel through China much more happily if you can see the haggling as a challenge that can give you pride and satisfaction too. Especially when you end up paying what you personally think the service or the item is worth to you, and when you regard the extra that has been squeezed out of you as your contribution towards the resolution of the North-South conflict. You might even have a lot of fun in the process, because in China conning foreigners goes hand-in-hand with laughing a lot. Just make a little effort and you will be rewarded. When I once ordered a bowl of noodles at a mooring on the Yangtse the cook grinned at me and said, 'Three yuan for you! If you hadn't spoken Chinese, I'd have charged you five.' We both laughed. I expect a Chinese would have only paid two yuan.

Secret tip 7

> You only have yourself to blame if you are
> as stupid as I was on that rickshaw trip.
> Negotiate all eventualities in advance,
> especially the price of goods or services.

On a personal level the Chinese are a wonderfully uncomplicated bunch of people. They are open, warm-hearted, curious and seldom grumpy. Here you don't have to look for a conversation, here conversations will find you. For chance meetings in the train or above pit toilets you should be ready to reveal where you are from, how old you are, if you are married and how much you earn. Your conversation partners will generally request the information in that order, before going on to discuss it at length in front of you to the person crouching at the next pit over. For more intimate conversations, also have at the ready your animal sign in the Chinese horoscope and your blood type. Not that you will be talking medical science necessarily, the Chinese just believe it helps them to get a good picture of you. Your blood type is said to reveal your character. You are ridiculously self-confident? Blood group O, no doubt. If other people always take advantage of you, you must be B.

New arrivals to China love to listen to those 'ah', 'aiyo', 'mmm' and 'ng' sounds of varying tone, modulation and length the Chinese are always uttering. They sometimes come in a guttural whisper, sometimes in more staccato manner. The Chinese love to sprinkle them as liberally in general conversation as they sprinkle peanuts onto Gongbao chicken. Much more than in European languages, these sounds are living organisms of agreement, astonishment and sympathy with a great many shades of meaning in between. This element of Chinese is particularly prevalent during phone conversations, leading a fascinated Irish friend of mine to coin his own term. He calls it 'unenthusiastic phone sex'.

Secret tip 8: For old-school Maoists

As soon as you land in Beijing, get a taxi, cover the windows and ask to be driven straight to the train station. From there, catch the next train to Pyongyang (Monday to Friday, departure time: 15:30).

Secret tip 9: For those tired of China

Ditto. One week in Pyongyang should be enough. Alternatively, try a month in Peterborough, Great Yarmouth or Leeds. You will soon feel that burning desire to return to Beijing.

Secret tip 10: If you miss China

To recreate the atmosphere of Beijing or Lanzhou as authentically as possible, lay a pipe from your living room to your garage. Close the garage door, start your car's engine and watch nostalgically as clouds of smoke fill your room. Then fetch your last bottle of Erguotou, some ink and a brush. Compose a poem to the little white clouds that are now hovering over your sofa.

Leave a red thermos flask decorated with peonies in every room. Pour yourself

a cup of lukewarm water every few hours
from one of them. After every sip smack
your lips and allow a pleasurable 'ahhh!' to
emanate from the depths of your soul.

Be nice to foreigners.

If you are still missing China after that
Then read. The following authors are worth scouring
second-hand bookshops for.

Carl Crow: An American adman whose book *Four
Hundred Million Customers* told people of life in 1930s'
Shanghai. Funny and eye-opening.

Lu Xun: If any Chinese author deserved to win the
Nobel Prize it is him. With a clear and lyrical eye,
his razor-sharp and melancholy short stories perfectly
dissected Chinese society. He was lucky to die before
the Communists took power.

Qian Zhongshu: Like Lu Xun, a 20th-century Chinese
author of world-class literature. He knew the West as

well as he knew the East, was a master of irony as well as of philosophy. In 1947 he wrote his satirical masterpiece *Fortress Besieged*.

Jonathan Spence: A sinologist who has mastered the art of both being scholarly and still writing vivid and enthralling books. He has written many bestsellers, all of which are recommended. *The Search for Modern China* is a classic.

Yan-Kit So: She wrote some of the best Chinese cookery books available in English. The food will taste just like it does in China. Buy one. Cook. Miss China even more.

终 **Zhong**

The end

In China it is rarely happy.
    (Closing line for pessimists).
And rarely is it the end.
    (Closing line for optimists).